Lost Cause

LOST CAUSE

Managing Poor Performers

XAVIER ZINN

Lost Cause: Managing Poor Performers

Published by Wheatmark®
1760 East River Road, Suite 145
Tucson, Arizona 85718 U.S.A.
www.wheatmark.com

ISBN: 978-1-60494-814-1
LCCN: 2013936621

Contents

Introduction

At one organization where I worked, we hired what we thought was a bright young person right out of a well-known MBA program. Based on his interviews, we thought "Kevin" (not his real name) would be capable of performing exceptionally, and he was given a job of some significance. Everyone involved considered Kevin's MBA degree a big plus and an indication that he had a substantial level of potential. Reality, however, was a much different story. As an aside, when I was hired at this company, they stated a number of times that they were a performance driven company. As it turned out, there was nothing performance driven about them. In many ways, the company encouraged the very poor standards of work I saw while I was there.

With a signing bonus and a $65,000 dollar-a-year salary, Kevin spent his first month in training. All staff in this position were trained extensively because they were doing some extremely important number crunching, and if they got it wrong it could mean the difference between profit and loss. After training, the new recruits were sent out to their various teams and started work. After three months—the usual probationary time for new employees—came their first review. Kevin's review was done by his current manager, who found him wanting in many respects. But instead of exercising his rights and letting Kevin go during his probationary period so he could hire someone better, this manager said, "Let's wait a little longer and see if Kevin comes into his own."

At the six-month mark, there was the first official performance management meeting with all the managers and directors of the department: one vice president, four directors, about fifteen managers, and one human resources representative all in a room ready to talk about seventy-five or so people. For each person, we would discuss their behaviour, ability, attitude, and potential. All this would be covered in three hours, so staying on track was paramount if we were to get everything done.

The first half of the meeting was moving along nicely; we managed to get through about half the managers. Each would give a short synopsis of her employees and their performance: just enough information to give everyone the gist of what was going on with that person. Then the wheels fell off the meeting. The next manager up started hemming and hawing about this particular employee, Kevin. He just couldn't seem to get the nuances of the job, and his pure analytical numbers skills, which were a very large part of the job, were lacking. Numerous times Kevin's work needed to be redone or given to someone else to check. You know it's a bad situation when a non-number cruncher looks at the numbers and says, "This doesn't look right." Kevin was always very apologetic about his lack of ability, but he never seemed to think he needed to improve. When he was offered remedial training, he accepted but never attended.

We wasted more than twenty minutes of that three-hour meeting discussing Kevin: how he did not understand the work, didn't provide the level of analysis needed and was generally failing. Some people, especially his current manager, felt that because of his MBA, Kevin must have the capacity to do better and that it must somehow be the actual work or the environment that was causing the issue. And yet Kevin's peers could understand and provide the needed analysis without any problems.[1]

Finally, somebody asked, "Does this person have the horsepower to get the job done?" The manager's answer was a mousy "I don't know." And as if this response wasn't baffling enough, a few minutes later, I heard Kevin's manager say to another manager, "I'm glad we're rotating responsibilities at the end of the month. Now a fresh set of eyes can be used to make a determination of Kevin's abilities." Six months later, the company did its official end-of-year performance evaluations to determine raises and bonuses. Kevin got a poor rating from his new manager as well, but he still got a raise and a bonus—albeit a smaller one than he would have gotten with a satisfactory rating. In twelve months, Kevin had gotten three evaluations that said his performance didn't meet his manager's expectations, and the only thing that happened was that his performance rating was poor.

At this point, most companies will put such a worker on a performance improvement plan, or at the very least provide some sort of help if they weren't terminated first. Not here. Kevin got another six months to see if he really couldn't do the job. It got to the point where all the managers in the company knew about Kevin, and were getting curious about the outcome of a situation that had gone on for so long. Finally, after about 16 months, we had another meeting. It was obvious—not that it hadn't already been obvious in the preceding 13 months— Kevin couldn't do the job. Termination was finally on the table. But instead of being fired, Kevin was given a couple of months to look for a new job—on company time. I suppose you could chalk that up to the company trying to be decent. The problem was the endless rationalization and the hope against hope that Kevin would become what they still thought he could be—a great employee. I was baffled by the situation. To me, and to a few other managers, it was painfully obvious that Kevin didn't

---

1   None of Kevin's peers had an MBA, and their start dates were the same.

have the ability to do this job, and since that's what he'd been hired for it seemed equally obvious that he should be terminated.

That meeting was the straw that broke the camel's back. After wasting my entire morning, the more I thought about the conversation we'd just had, the more annoyed I became. By the time I got back to my office, I had decided that this bothered me so greatly I had no alternative but to write this book.

This book is the result of years of dealing with poor performers at all levels of the organizations I have worked at. After this episode, I started observing in a very critical way how we as managers judge, rate, and manage staff. Managers can convince themselves that an employee's poor performance is up them to fix, and it's not the employee's responsibility. I finally realized there is an unwritten rule in business: everyone is capable of meeting anyone's expectations. The thinking behind this idea is something like this: if someone cannot reach a certain standard, there must be some external reason, and if you can find and fix that problem you'll get the right level of performance out of your staff. The reason for this thinking is obvious when you consider that management deals mostly with external variables.[2] This leads managers to think the problem of poor performance can be solved like so many other problems—by changing or modifying the various external variables.

When people perform badly, we tend to look around for outside explanations. I put the responsibility back where it belongs—squarely on the worker. Once we identify the worker and not the workplace as the problem, the question of how to manage the poor performer becomes effectively irrelevant. More than likely, very little improvement is possible so what can be done? Your staff's performance can be tempered with the

---

2   "This may be childishly obvious, but the major approaches to managing the worker, throughout history, have focused on elements external to the job." Drucker, Peter F. *The Frontiers of Management: Where Tomorrow's Decisions Are Being Shaped Today.* New York: Truman Talley, 1986. p. 188.

right development, but is development to bring someone up to the minimum standard a good use of resources? To those who think so, I ask: if you hire someone to do a job, shouldn't that person have the skills to do that job? How can anyone say it's all right for workers to need remedial training to get the skills they should already have to perform their job function?

We rate a person's workplace performance against some set of criteria. In this book, we are not interested in people who meet or exceed the given criteria; the people we are interested in are those who cannot reach an acceptable level of performance, who have never, or only sporadically, achieved the minimum performance standard. We are interested in the chronic, or true, poor performer.

In the business world, once a chronic poor performer is identified, a certain mindset takes over. All sensible thinking stops, and blind allegiance to commonly accepted practices dictates that everyone can succeed if only they are given the right management. Only after many tries have failed does the manager admit that maybe that person is not capable and begin the long process of getting the performance problem "officially" certified. Only then can we do something about it.

Terminating an employee for performance reasons has become so difficult that it is effectively not an option. What happens instead is that poor performers either keep their jobs or get shuffled to other positions where they also perform badly.[3] We claim that a business is not a charity, but when it comes to the staff, this is not entirely correct. Companies throughout the world employ people who by every objective measure are poor performers, but for some reason, they are reluctant to dismiss these people and hire better talent. Why is management so

---

3   The funny thing about all of the things we do regarding poor performers is that it continues to enable the poor performance. Parham, Creda, Pamler Joe. "The Construct of Substance Abuse Enabling Applied to Poor Performance Management: How Managers Deal with Poor Performing Employees." Virginia Polytechnic Institute and State University, 2003. United States—Virginia: 50–52.

averse to realizing the obvious and acting to correct the situation? It is one thing not to notice poor performance; it is quite another to notice it, assess it, and still decide that tolerating the problem is better than removing the problem. Only in business does this type of logic prevail, and generally speaking, it does not make sense.

Dealing with a poor performer is painful. Frustration and stress run surprisingly high, and your patience can be surprisingly low, especially when something needs to be done about that person's performance and you are the manager. But how does anyone expect things to change when a poor performer can continue working without improving and at the end of the year, can still get an increase because "everyone else got one."[4] Has anyone thought about the damage this can do to the psyche of a company? Is it wise not to package someone out just because you don't like the idea of "paying him to leave"? Instead, this thinking leads the company to spend time, effort, and money on people who will never repay the investment. How does this make sense?

This book is not about firing a poor performer—although that's often the only option. It's about how companies blindly deal with poor performers. It is obvious to me we have institutionalized the problem of poor performance because of our flawed assumptions about reaching expectations. When we look at the current practices for getting a poor performer on track, I think it will be obvious to you too. My hope is that this book will provide a different perspective on a problem that pervades business by raising questions, enlightening managers, and challenging the current thinking.

---

4   See table 5.2 on page 74 for a list of enabling behaviours for poor performers in Parham, Creda, Pamler, Joe. "The Construct of Substance Abuse Enabling Applied to Poor Performance Management: How Managers Deal with Poor Performing Employees." Virginia Polytechnic Institute and State University, 2003. United States—Virginia:

Lost Cause

1

Do You Have a Poor Performer?

What Is a Poor Performer?

A Definition

What is poor performance? We all know it when we see it, but can we define it? *Poor*[1] simply means "less than good"; *Performance*[2] is activity that can be measured and judged. The person who performs that activity is the performer.[3]

These are simple concepts, but at least this gives us a definition to use as a starting point for discussing poor performance. When we combine the words "poor" and "performance," we

---

1 Poor: "less good than usual or expected; of little excellence or worth; inferior, paltry" *New Shorter Oxford English Dictionary.*

2 Performance: "the execution or accomplishment of an action, operation, or process undertaken or ordered; the doing of any action or work, the quality of this especially as observable under particular conditions." *New Shorter Oxford English Dictionary.*

3 Performer: "a person who carries out or executes an undertaking, action, etc., especially in a specified manner" *New Shorter Oxford English Dictionary.*

get a term that means: actions, tasks, or operations executed in a manner that is lower than the expected level of care, quality, and speed.[4] Competent people may perform poorly because of a setback in their lives, but these are not the people I am talking about. I am talking about the chronic poor performer— the person who has never achieved an acceptable performance rating in her career, yet still manages to be employed.

In some jobs, like professional sports for instance, it is easy to see poor performance. If a team loses by a wide margin, the team, or a certain player, probably played badly. The lost game is evidence of poor task execution or not performing to an acceptable standard. In the business world, poor performance may not be as obvious, especially to employees who do not work directly with the poor performer. As well, poor performance can also take on different manifestations such as: an extended due date, a reduction in project scope, or greater resources required for a given project or task. The issue is further clouded because terms like "productivity," "quality," and "output" mean different things to different people and a lack of standardized definitions[5] can be part of the problem, although I can't believe something like this is a major factor in many cases.

In a business environment, you want speedy output of high-quality work. You consider one person to be better than another when he is faster at producing the same thing with the

4   We can consider this our definition of poor performance or interchange it with "the failure of an employee to do the job at an acceptable level . . . typically defined in terms of quality, quantity, or timeliness," since you will hear that type of saying throughout the book as well. Parham, Creda Pamler Joe. "The Construct of Substance Abuse Enabling Applied to Poor Performance Management: How Managers Deal with Poor Performing Employees." PhD diss., Virginia Polytechnic Institute and State University, 2003. You can also find this definition at http://www.opm. gov/er/poor/understanding.asp.

5   After the fact performance definitions and varying interpretations are part of the problem. Latham, G. P., L. L. Cummings, and T. R. Mitchell. "Behavioral Strategies to Improve Productivity." *Organizational Dynamics*, 9(3):4–23.

same quality. If someone can simultaneously do multiple things while maintaining high output and quality, even better. Ideally, you want all your staff to be high performers with high multitasking abilities.

Some Traits of the Poor Performer

From my observations poor performers typically produce lower-quality work, and do their work more slowly than others. Over the years these are some of the traits that I have observed in poor performers:[6]

- poor time management stemming from poor priority-setting
- lack of urgency in doing their tasks
- an inflated perception of their own importance and abilities
- a belief that everyone else is the problem
- generally poor cognitive and communication skills, including difficulty interpreting instructions
- poor multitasking skills
- generally slow in doing their work

They also lack initiative and appear to be overwhelmed substantially more than anyone else. This usually leads to "the everything is difficult" syndrome, which is fed by their amazing ability to complicate things unnecessarily. Poor performers are unable to distinguish between what is trivial and what is important, which causes problems with time management. This creates a vicious circle where one behaviour feeds another, creating the very situation they find themselves in.

Good performers prioritize their time and workload; poor performers can't or don't. Poor performers can always find time

---

6 For a truly complete list, see the nine pages of behaviours Pamela Levine came up with in *Substandard Job Performance: Development of a Model and the Examination of Poor Organizational Performers*. Colorado State University, 2006.

to go to company lunches, outings, and anything that is fun and not work related, but they cannot meet their manager's expectations. If you point out that they are missing your deadlines or the quality of their work is not up to standard, they claim to be overworked or that the deadline is too aggressive. They don't think of working harder to meet the deadline because in their eyes they are already working at full capacity. There is a disconnect between their actual output and what they think they are doing and this usually stems from a distorted perception of who they are and what they can do. If the poor performer is likeable and can convince her manager she is capable, the manager will invariably cut her some slack even if her skills are not adequate.[7] Only after a significant amount of time will the manager eventually ask if this person is ever going to get it.

Poor performers come in all shapes and sizes with all manner of bad work habits; some get overwhelmed easily, others think they can do everything, others are lazy, others are slow. The list goes on. My definition is: A poor performer is someone whose actions, tasks, or operations are done in a manner that is much lower than the expected standard. Everyone has demonstrated at least one, if not all, of the traits listed earlier at some point in their careers. What distinguishes poor performers is that they show most of these traits, and they do not seem interested in improving those things a manager deems negative.

What a Poor Performer Is Not

Two types of problem employees are sometimes mistakenly lumped together with poor performers: the slacker and the employee with a bad attitude.

If you can put the fear of God into someone and get

---

7   This is just another example of confirmation bias. According to Robert Sutton, "Confirmation bias can causes bosses to make glowing judgments about people . . . they simply find to be likeable or admirable." Sutton, Robert I. *Good Boss, Bad Boss: How to Be the Best . . . and Learn from the Worst*. New York: Business Plus, 2010. p. 117.

them to perform to your standards, you don't have a true poor performer, you have a slacker—someone who does the bare minimum because she can get away with it. People tend to assume that poor performers are slackers, which leads them to believe that the employee will fall in line after an appropriate reprimand. But as we will soon see, this is only possible with employees who are capable of doing their work, and not everyone is.

A bad attitude does not make a poor performer either. If the person can get the job done, and you can tolerate his attitude, then you don't have a poor performer, you have a pain in the ass. If you cannot deal with his attitude, he is not an organizational fit. This gets lumped into poor performance because where else would you put it? A bad organizational fit can manifest itself as poor performance or other negative behaviour, but for the most part it feeds into the assumption that everyone is capable of reaching any standard and an external force is the cause of the poor performance. In the case of a true poor performer, this is just more smoke overlaying the real issue.

Measuring Performance

Perception of Performance

The funny thing about performance is that although it is assessed differently for every job position,[8] collectively people are more than capable of determining who the strong performers are and who are the weak performers. This is not because people use special information to make these determinations: they inherently know when they observe the workers around them.

Sports are the easiest way to illustrate this. When you watch the Olympics, it's very easy to tell who the best athletes are; they're the ones who are winning. The best athletes from each

---

8   Latham, G. P., L. L. Cummings, and T. R. Mitchell. "Behavioral Strategies to Improve Productivity." *Organizational Dynamics*, 9(3):4–23.

country are sent to the Olympics, but it's not until we bring them together that we see who the absolute best are. The people bringing up the rear are obviously not in the same league as the person who wins, and that is what we need to remember here. Not everyone can win, so do we really want to spend an enormous amount of time effort and money on the ones who will never be able to win, or do we want to continue to improve those who have the potential to win?

Using Performance Metrics

The perception of poor performance is a little more nebulous in the business world. Although it is easy to form an intuitive assessment of employee performance, there are several reasons why we are not always objective,[9] especially when performance is poor. Sometimes managers expect too much, or the employee does not have a clear understanding of the expectations, so it is incumbent on the manager to ensure that expectations are clear and performance is measured effectively. Although most of your performance assessment is done by informal observation and conversation, you can't see in black and white that someone is not performing until you have objective data.[10]

---

9   Confirmation bias is what this is all about. Basically, "one tends to notice and to look for what confirms one's beliefs and to ignore, not look for, or undervalue the relevance of what contradicts one's beliefs." Sutton, Robert I. *Good Boss, Bad Boss: How to Be the Best . . . and Learn from the Worst.* New York: Business Plus, 2010. p. 117.

10   Although clear-cut is sometimes not so clear-cut, I don't think it is unreasonable for a manager to say, "do a good job" and have the receiving party on some visceral level understand what "do a good job" means, even if it is not articulated in the appropriate manner.

Defining Meaningful Metrics

What are metrics?[11] We've all heard the word—maybe even defined a few of these as well—but do we really understand what we are doing when it comes to metrics? If we measured productivity by counting keystrokes, we might conclude that someone really has her nose to the grindstone when really she just left a book on the keyboard when she left for lunch. A manager might say after looking at the keystroke metric, "Holy cow, you're right! How could I have been so foolish as to think you were just a poor performer! It's entirely my fault, and I apologize. You'll get a new person tomorrow!"

What's the probability of this happening? Exactly zero. But it does bring up an important point: metrics need to be meaningful and purposeful. Metrics essentially measure a factor that people think is important to determine a multitude of things.

You could view metrics as being part of an SLA (service level agreement) of sorts. The problem with our earlier example is that keystrokes are not very relevant to job tasks. This is the problem with metrics: metrics that are easy to measure are often poor measures of job performance.[12] What would be a meaningful metric to measure the success of a help desk? Does it make sense to use the number of tickets the help desk processes per day or week?

Here there seems to be a disconnect. If there was a metric to measure the percentage of tickets closed by the help desk on the first call, this would be a suitable measurement, not only to the managers of the help desk but also to the employees who

---

11 The definition I came up with and use is: metrics—an important defined measure used to ensure the quality or quantity of something within a prescribed timeline. The dictionary states: "a method of measuring something, or the results obtained from this." *New Shorter Oxford English Dictionary.*

12 "Get the metrics wrong and unintended behavior is the result" Taptiklis, T. "After Managerialism." *Emergence: Complexity & Organization,* 7(3/4):2–14.

call the help desk. If an SLA says the help desk will rectify 80% of all incidents on the first call and the help desk was reaching, say, 92%, that would indicate that the help desk was doing its job regarding that SLA. That metric is relevant to a relevant SLA. When somebody complains that the help desk "sucks," the help desk managers can pull these numbers out and show that the help desk is meeting or exceeding the applicable SLA. Even better: these numbers should be posted so everyone knows how the help desk is doing. Conversely, when metrics measure the wrong thing, like length of call time in the belief that the shorter the call the better the service, very strange things can begin to happen.

When we define an SLA, there should metrics to measure against it. Problems occur when SLAs and metrics do not jibe. A server uptime level of 99.999% is useless if people don't have access to the server. Having the wrong metrics can create a blame game that wastes time instead of addressing the real problem.

You cannot measure something when you don't know what you want to get out of it or what purpose it will serve. Metrics for metrics' sake serve no purpose either. To get meaningful metrics, you must understand what you are trying to achieve from an overall perspective and determine whether metrics can help with that. If you wanted to understand your call times, it would make sense to have a call time metric, but what purpose would that serve? You would not be looking at the problem but at a symptom of something else. The problem you are trying to solve is at a higher level. Let's say you wanted to increase call responsiveness by a certain amount. Some of the metrics you would need to would be call times, number of calls, number of staff available, number of calls per staff, number of calls/hour, types of issues, average time to deal with those issues, etc. The point of this information is to help you solve your problem: increase call responsiveness by X percent.

Good metrics don't just quantify results; they help identify bottlenecks, problems, and potential solutions. Maybe you find that customer service takes 75% of the calls from 8 am to 2 pm. The average call duration is 9 minutes, and 70% of your calls relate to one particular issue. It may be possible to rearrange the work schedule, create a new process or modify an existing one, or explain your findings and get that particular problem the attention it deserves so it can be fixed properly. As you can see, this is substantially more helpful that just getting numbers for call times.

Metrics can make your life miserable if the design is poor, the purpose is not entirely applicable based on the metrics, or the measures are wrong. Remember: "not everything that can be counted counts and not everything that counts can be counted."[13]

It is also very possible to corrupt the entire purpose as well. How would you increase customer responsiveness if you were the help desk for instance? Well, one very easy way would be to send an email to each person who contacts the help desk with a stated SLA, i.e., "You will be contacted within X hours about your issue." Although you have met the stated goal, you have not done anything of substance. As Jeffery Pfeffer and Robert Sutton say: "By focusing only on what can be quantified, we can lose sight of what matters most."[14]

Measuring Poor Performers

What does all this have to do with our poor performers? Well, to measure their abilities and capabilities against others, we need to understand what we are trying to do with the information. Is the purpose to get evidence of their poor performance, or is it to help them reach the same level as others doing

---

13   Quoted from Einstein. Pfeffer, Jeffrey, and Robert I. Sutton. *Hard Facts, Dangerous Half-Truths, and Total Nonsense: Profiting from Evidence-Based Management.* Boston, MA: Harvard Business School, 2006. p. 40.

14   Pfeffer, Jeffrey, and Robert I. Sutton. *Hard Facts, Dangerous Half-Truths, and Total Nonsense: Profiting from Evidence-Based Management.* Boston, MA: Harvard Business School, 2006.

the same job, or is it something different yet again? If they are poor performers, you probably already know they are,[15] but how poor are they really? The metrics you need to determine this are many, but what do you do when everyone you manage is poor, or only slightly better than the poorest one on the team? This is where SLAs help by defining the standard and the criteria for the measurement. This is important to remember because a well-crafted SLA can make your job substantially easier when it comes to measuring employee performance. If the employees fail the standard, it is not the manager's standard but rather the standard defined by the business.

Are metrics useful? In the end, all that even the best metrics can do is measure. They may help you get some people to work harder or more effectively, but for poor performers all metrics will do is show in glaring detail how poor they really are. They may improve marginally,[16] but even that will be temporary.

From my experience, very rarely do we use metrics to promote the positive. Instead, they are a way to show some type of problem that needs to be addressed. "You need to bring your numbers up 15%" for instance. Regarding people; you can't just measure your poor performers because that would be singling out some of your staff. To be fair, you have to measure everyone, which means you may insult your high performers by measuring them when they are meeting or exceeding requirements.

We determine that there is some type of performance issue, and by measuring the various aspects of that problem we believe we can identify the cause. Although metrics do have a place in business and they do offer information you can act on provided they measure the right thing the right way, it is unfortunate that many people think metrics will somehow cause the

---

15 Be careful about confirmation bias you may be feeding into your own assumptions.

16 I would attribute the increase in performance to the Hawthorne Effect. The improvement is only happening because performance is now being monitored, and after some period of time the performance will be back to where it once was.

poor performer to pull up his socks and permanently improve. That's like expecting an oil well to produce more oil once you measure it.

What Are an Employee's Obligations?

Fulfilling the Employment Contract

What are an employee's obligations to the employer? Other than the obvious, such as being punctual, what else are employees obliged to do? I would say their obligation is to do the job to the best of their ability, or at the very least be acceptable. Acceptable performance can be defined with metrics or other measurable criteria; the point is that employees know what is expected in the job. When people know what's expectated, do they make sure they perform to an acceptable level? It is a simple question, and although the answer should be yes, with poor performers we know that it is usually no.

Instinctively, we all know that we should do a good job. How many people think to themselves, "I will do a poor job" on something they are responsible for? Remember, there is a contract between the employee and the employer: the job description. Unfortunately, the job description falls short in one important way: although it defines what people will do in their jobs, it stops short of setting concrete standards for fulfilling those tasks.

Once employed, a worker should know what his manager expects of them and also how he will achieve it. If he needs to work late, he works late. If he needs to start early, he comes in early. If he needs help, he asks for it. If the employee can't or doesn't know how to meet the expectation, how can someone honestly say he's performing adequately in his position? And if he's not performing adequately, isn't the entire employment contract now up in the air? The employer is giving this person a salary to do a job, and the employee has to maintain his end of the bargain.

Imagine if a business only paid its workers a percentage of their salaries every pay period because it just could not manage to pay the entire amount; how would the workers feel? How long would they stick around? They would not give the company too many chances, nor would anybody suggest that the company take sensitivity training for this behaviour. Yes, this analogy sounds a little ridiculous, yet companies do something very similar for workers who do not meet expectations. To take it further, imagine this scenario: an employee wants to quit because the company cannot pay her salary on time, but instead of putting in her resignation, she talks to HR and sets up a three-month payment schedule with the employer to complete the objectives of paying her what is owed every pay period. Obviously, we don't do that—yet this is the process with a poor performer. Employment is a two-way street, and both sides need to meet expectations. If this is not happening, it says to me that the original employment contract is null and void.

Is it the manager's responsibility to tell an employee how to achieve an acceptable level? Let's say for the sake of argument that there is a genuine issue that needs to be resolved, and an employee asks you, his manager, "How do I achieve an acceptable level?" You outline your expectations, the objectives that need to be hit, help him with contacts, process any documents he needs, explain how the company operates, and give him any other relevant information he needs. Looking for direction is fine,[17] but if an employee wants to be told exactly what to do and how to do it, that's a problem. It suggests that a person doesn't want to think for himself, and doesn't want to take responsibility for his actions. "My manager told me to do this," will be constantly heard in the corridors of the office. Is this

---

17   In situational leadership, there is the concept of development level of staff (D1–D4) and the four leadership styles (S1–S4). These can be put in a matrix chart to determine the best way to manage various types of people. Ideally you do not want D1's or D2's for long, you want staff to move into D3 and D4. See: Shive, Cody B. *Technical Management with Situational Leadership*. The Arrington Group.

person an asset to the company? Is that an acceptable level of performance?

An employee should have the skills to do her job and the intelligence to fulfill her objectives with the appropriate level of care and an acceptable level of quality in the allotted time. That is expected, regardless of the task, and the employee needs to figure out how to do that. If she can't figure out how to do her job, is she meeting the acceptable level expectation? This may sound harsh, but when you hired the person what was your expectation? Did the manager expect to have to outline in detail every aspect of how the job should be done or did he expect that the person hired for the job would know how to get things done? I would say almost everyone expects the latter. If a worker needs an unreasonable amount of supervision, the contract you agreed to is not being upheld.

Special problems can arise if managers direct their staff in too much detail. Some managers prefer to tell their staff how to do something and when to do it (also known as micromanaging). Are staff still responsible for meeting their objectives if a manager tells them how to do their job and when? What if the manager tells them to do something that is not on their objectives and because of that they cannot meet acceptable criteria? Whose fault is that? Will the manager take responsibility, or should the blame be on the shoulders of the staff members who could not meet the expectation?

Like most, I would expect staff members to handle both their objectives and their manager's other requests. A high performer would do both just because that is who he is; an average performer would more than likely accomplish both as well. Employees in those two groups would at least ask clarifying questions to identify priorities. Poor performers, on the other hand, would not be able to do both. Whose fault is the failure? Here, I would say the manager because she should have known better than to offer more work to an employee who is on the trailing edge of performance.

This might make sense if your goal was to continually

enforce the fact that your poor performer cannot perform, but if your goal is to get things done, give the special projects to people who you know can complete them on top of everything else they are responsible for. Developing staff and pushing them to do more is fine if they are capable and willing; if they are not you cannot force them. Your poor performers will continue to fail, and you will fail along with them if you think you can manage them to become better.

You can "work smart not hard" by looking for the most efficient way to get something done. Time is a constant resource: you can't slow time down, but you can accomplish more in the same amount of time if you think about what you need to do and how to do it. There are times when you just have to bust your ass to get a thing done, and that's fine. But other times you can look at a situation and realize that either the process has broken or there is an easier way to do something and get the same result. In my experience, poor performers do not think this way. They follow a process, whether it's right or wrong, and do not bother to understand what purpose it serves in the grand scheme of things.

Let's say an employee had to transfer boxes from one side of a warehouse to the other. The current process is to pick up one box at a time and carry to the other side. It takes eight hours to move all the boxes from one side to the other. What would a poor performer do? Maybe get a skid and put multiple boxes on it and drag it over? Perhaps he would get a forklift to move the boxes more easily. This makes sense; most people would figure out a way to make that job easier. The question we need to ask is, why do the boxes need to be moved over to the other side? What purpose does this process serve?

There may be a perfectly good reason the boxes have to move to the other side of the warehouse, but often there is not. How many times has someone said to you, "It was like that when I got here," or, "This is the way I was taught." How many processes have you personally followed without asking why? If we ask questions about why this task is necessary or what purpose it serves, we may find a solution to the "problem" that is more efficient and makes more sense than the one currently being followed. By asking questions and understanding what purpose the process serves, an employee can understand how it is possible to modify the process to achieve the business's goals in less time. Now that they have cut down the time it takes to get that task completed, they can do other things—which are probably more important. Efficiency is something business likes, and if it is possible to find more efficient methods, it is unlikely those suggestions will meet resistance.

Invisible Expectations and Adding Value

I do not think it is unreasonable for an employer to expect an employee to do his best every day. I know this is not possible, especially in an office environment, but it is possible to try. Some days a worker's best is completely over the top; other days it just barely covers what is necessary. But over the course of a year, the good should outweigh the bad, resulting in acceptable performance over the year.

What does the worker think her obligation is? Is it to do the bare minimum for the wage provided? Someone who says, "I just want to do my job and nothing else" needs to learn that there is something else; she needs to learn on the job. A worker needs to upgrade her skills on her own. She needs to do more than what people expect of her and what her job description says. She needs to understand the politics, the business, and her place in it. She has to understand that presidents and VPs get special treatment—these are the facts of life in every company— and understanding this is also rolled up in the expectations that employers have of every one of their staff. If a worker does any less, people will consider her difficult, self-absorbed, not a team player, and generally a poor organizational fit compared to those who can do these invisible things.

So what does it really mean to perform to an acceptable level? It means doing the job to an acceptable level, and meeting the invisible expectations too. Each worker is interacting with human beings all day every day, and sometimes how he interacts with others says more about his capabilities than his actual job performance. If people perceive a worker as a good person, eager to help and willing to do more, his performance does not have to be stellar for him to be considered to be performing to expectation;[18] this person is "adding value," and the company likes that.

What is value added? Quite simply, it is those tasks the company does not pay an employee to do but that in some way help the company. Some people are on a million committees. Others are doing jobs that are out of scope for their role; still others are learning new jobs or skills. Each of these activities adds value to the company. A Christmas party doesn't happen out of thin air, does it? People who organize social events add value for the company because they save the company having to hire someone to do that job. If a desktop support person also does server upgrades and maintenance, she helps the company because it does not have to hire someone to do that work. The employee might eventually move into that role herself, so she is also helping herself in this instance. Is it not in the employee's best interests to perform some value-added work? The worker should see this as an opportunity instead of as a request for extra work without extra pay.

If a company hires someone to take out the garbage, but he can also fix a clogged sink and do the laundry, they would consider this worker to be adding value because he can do more than what he was hired for. Companies prefer to hire people who can offer value added services, because sometimes workers need to go outside the scope of their job descriptions to get the job done, and it saves time and money if workers have the flexibility to do so. So, all things being equal, would you hire

---

18   This pertains specifically to knowledge workers in an office environment. Other environments where quotas are implemented, for example, would require the person to achieve the quota as well as all the invisible things mentioned. Again, this pertains to confirmation bias.

someone who just took out the garbage, or someone who can do more than that? And would you keep someone who could not take out the garbage, or forgot half of it every week? Before we leave this subject, let me just say this: I am not suggesting we must base everything on the fastest work and the highest productivity. But efficiency is important. If someone can do two things (to an acceptable standard of quality, of course) against someone else's one, that person is better. Does that mean you should work your staff to death? No, but when someone can do more in a given time, you, as the manager, have options. You can opt to increase output, or you can opt to let those staff members do other things outside their daily tasks if they are interested and the business is willing to support it. Does a poor performer have the time to do this when she is not meeting her targets, quotas, and timelines? It does not appear so.

Value added work is a beautiful thing. You get more out of your staff than what their job descriptions say, and your staff gets the benefit of a new set of skills and experiences if they are willing to see it that way. But here is the catch: is there compensation for this value added work? "Compensation" is an interesting word. Most of us take it to mean more money—let's face it, a new job title does not pay the bills. Keep in mind that compensation is not a magic bullet, and even if you do compensate people properly, it is still possible for them to be dissatisfied with that compensation.

2

Reasons for Poor Performance

Do You Have a Culture of Mediocrity? The Contribution of Workplace Culture

I am sure you have a list of people you would hire in a heartbeat if the opportunity presented itself. The people on your list either meet or exceed those criteria you find important. Everyone maintains this list of absolute performance, which ranks everybody you have worked with throughout your career. Bill from company A is better than John from company B, but Karen from company C is better than both, etc.

As you move around, you may notice that someone who others consider a top performer in organization A would be an average performer in organization B. We do this every day, and there is nothing wrong with this. The problem arises when you base your expectations of your employees on the performance of staff that you worked with at other companies. What you consider a poor performer could be your new company's average performer. Whatever the situation, it is obvious your relative perceptions need to be brought in line with your company's understanding of performance and what criteria define poor, average, and exceptional. When we do individual performance ratings, we don't rate our staff against people in other companies, so it is quite possible for the top performers in two different organizations to be vastly different on an absolute scale.

As a manager, you will have to adjust your perceptions to work within the reality of the current organization. If you push your staff to achieve your version of good performance, based on another company's standards, you will probably antagonize them.[1] Culture drives how a company operates, and it is very powerful. If you oppose it, you will fail and be very, very frustrated. You need to be aware of the company culture and know what is acceptable and what is not. Coming in with grand ideas and pushing everyone to be better, faster, and smarter may make you look good, or it may backfire and leave you burnt out and defeated. If the organization is happy with the current performance level of your department, all you're doing is making yourself look good on the backs of your staff because you're not fixing a problem in the company's eyes.

If you move to a new company and the mandate there is to move to a more intense and performance-driven culture, or even to improve the performance of a department just a little, you have the latitude to do what's necessary to accomplish that goal. If, however, you arrive and everything is plodding along with no overt complaints, and the business is happy or indifferent with the current level of commitment and expertise from its staff, although it is woefully less than what you have experienced or want, you need to make a decision about your future. What alternatives do you have? Well, you have two options, most aptly put by The Clash in their song "Should I Stay or Should I Go." You can either stay and step in line with how

---

1   "A disagreement or a conflict is likely not to be the answers, or indeed about anything ostensible. It is, in most cases, the result of incongruity in perceptions." Drucker, Peter F. *The Frontiers of Management: Where Tomorrow's Decisions Are Being Shaped Today.* New York: Truman Talley, 1986.

the company operates, adjusting your performance expectations accordingly, or you can leave.

Depending where you are in your career, you may find that slowing down and riding out the job until retirement appeals to you. If it does not, then work at the job until you find something else and then leave. Don't feel guilty about not being able to change things in a positive way because the business will continue to function without you, in much the same way that you left it. Everyone is replaceable, and 10 minutes after you walk out the door they will forget about you—if you don't believe that, you're deluding yourself.

Lack of Capacity

What Is Natural Ability?

What do I mean by natural ability, also known as talent?[2] Do you know someone who can easily pick up almost anything and very quickly be more skilled than others without a lot of time, practice, or instruction? This is natural talent, and every single person has natural talent for every single thing; some just have more than others for a given task. Some people run faster than others, some people run farther, some people are adept at reading body language, others are good with numbers, and others still are smarter than the rest of us in a given subject; it is just the way it is. Through training you can become better and get closer to your personal theoretical maximum performance in a particular task, but you will never be able to exceed your natural limits, whatever they are.

Let's say a sprinter can run the 100-metre dash in 11 seconds. With training, hypnosis, and eating right, he can get to his best performance: say, 9.90 seconds. That's his limit.

---

2 Talent: "Mental endowment; natural ability . . . A special natural ability or aptitude for or for a given thing." *New Shorter Oxford English Dictionary*. I define it as a predetermined level of innate ability that augments performance in task execution.

He cannot achieve a faster time no matter what he does. If he alters the playing field and takes performance-enhancing drugs, he can get to 9.75 seconds, but even then there comes a point where he can't improve anymore. This is a world-class time, so is it possible for everyone on the planet to run this fast? No, and we accept that. On my best day, I couldn't break 12 seconds. Maybe with a few years of training, I could eventually reach 11 seconds or so, but would it make sense for me to go to the Olympics? Not unless humiliation was the point, because the bar is so far above what I am capable of doing there could be no competition. On that level my performance is not even close to acceptable.

When there is a level that needs to be reached, some people can reach it, and others cannot. Unfortunately, I am pretty sure using performance-enhancing drugs will not actually do anything of benefit for poor employees in the workplace. All people have is their natural talent, experience, training, and the skills they have learned along the way. Where they are is where they will be. Maybe you can squeeze another 5% out of them, but that is it: after that they are maxed out. Expecting anything more is cruel and unusual punishment.

Everyone has the ability to do anything in the world. The real question is: is everyone capable of achieving the requisite expectation for a particular task, whatever it is? I could perform brain surgery tomorrow, but do I have the knowledge and skills necessary to perform the tasks associated with brain surgery properly? As of the moment, no. So if the job I applied for said I needed to have those skills and knowledge, should I be hired or continue to be employed if there is no way I can acquire those skills and knowledge in a reasonable time frame? Of course not. This is what we need to keep in mind when we hire people: we expect that they are capable and have the requisite skills and knowledge to do the job they applied for.

Not All Employees Are Created Equal

The ability someone has is directly proportional to their potential[3]—excluding attitude, of course—and potential leads to capacity. Let's say you have two pitchers of water, each representing a person: one holds 500 ml and the other holds 750 ml. We fill each of the pitchers to the 300 ml mark. The volume of the pitcher not filled with fluid is its potential (currently unfulfilled capacity). Its ability, so to speak, is represented by the fluid filled to 300 ml. Clearly the 750 ml pitcher has more capacity, i.e., potential. The ability of the person represented by that pitcher must at some point become greater than that of the person represented by the 500 ml pitcher. Someone with more potential has a higher reserve—is capable of doing the same amount of work without the same effort expended. You could say this example is the difference between a high performer and a good performer. The poor performer would likely be a 250 ml container. His potential and ability are low compared with the other pitchers, so his working ability is at or near his potential. He is completely maxed out and cannot, no matter how much he tries, meet expectations.

There are many variables to consider, but I think it is safe to say no one wants to hire someone who will be maxed out on her potential and abilities when for the same price, or within degrees of that price, you could have someone with higher potential and ability. It is entirely possible for someone with high potential not to perform to our expectations, but when that happens, we say, "she didn't live up to her potential." We're disappointed when we think an employee could have achieved more, given our observations, remember Kevin from the beginning of the book? But if our staff have low potential, disappointment is guaranteed.

---

3   Potential: "that which is possible as opp. to actual; a possibility; spec. capacity for use or development, resources able to be used or developed." *New Shorter Oxford English Dictionary.*

Can a Poor Performer Become a Good Performer?

Obviously, something needs to be done if your staff cannot meet the company's needs, but what? I think you know, but we as managers apparently have to exhaust all avenues available to us before we can think about something as final as termination. I don't have a problem with this thinking entirely—only when it overrules common sense, which seems to be more often than not. If you want a diamond, you can either go to a jeweller and buy one to the specifications you require, or you can go and mine one yourself. Which makes more sense? Almost everyone will pick the former because that is the best use of resources and time.

A manager should look at their target and ask, do I have the people necessary to achieve that result? If the answer is yes, but the staff needs help, then provide the staff with the help they need. But if your answer is, no, I don't think so, then you have a problem. You need to make hard decisions because if you put your staff up for tasks they are not capable of doing, this will eventually reflect negatively on you and the rest of your staff when they need to meet timelines or provide results that affect other people. Don't waste time, money, or effort on staff when you know there is no value in doing so. But what do managers usually do when they realize none of their efforts are paying off? They try harder at managing and expect something different. Some would say that doing the same thing over and over again and expecting a different result is insanity. In business we call it managing, and sometimes it really does not make sense. Especially when you already know that you can't really get your staff to do anything to begin with!

What do we do as managers to make the situation better? We offer time management training, technical training, team morale exercises, management meetings, and so on. Is that looking at the situation objectively? Is it possible that some people are just better than others? If that is the case, why do we constantly attempt to bring those poor performers in line with a performance expectation we know they can never reach?[4] Is it because we believe that if we manage them properly, they will suddenly blossom and become great[5], or is it because in the world of business this is the accepted way of doing things, and as long as a manager does all the "right" things, we consider that person's poor performance not the manager's fault?

Even if poor performers are capable of receiving feedback and improving their work, how much are they truly going to improve? Improving by, say, 5% may be good on paper, but if they were working at 40% and are now at 45%, is that good? It is an improvement, but it is still poor by any standard. Is it enough of an improvement to continue to be employed?

The Role of Passion: Are Poor Performers Just in the Wrong Place?

I think we can generally agree that if a person is passionate about something, she will typically work better at that task because she enjoys it. We have all heard people say that you

---

4   In *First, Break All the Rules*, the concept of non-talent and weakness is discussed. To them, "A nontalent becomes a weakness when you find yourself in a role where success depends on your excelling in an area that is a nontalent." I think this defines the problem well. The solution is to "devise a support system. Find a complementary partner. Or find an alternative role." You will see later that this definition really is geared toward people who are competent and are capable but are faltering. This is not designed to treat true poor performance, although they do mention on page 174 in the last paragraph that if the poor performance is continual then you have made a "casting error" and "at this point it is time to fix the casting error and to stop trying to fix the person." Buckingham, Marcus, and Curt Coffman. *First, Break All the Rules: What the World's Greatest Managers Do Differently*. New York, NY: Simon & Schuster, 1999. p. 167–178.

5   Michael Schrage says, "A collaboration of incompetents, no matter how diligent or well-meaning, cannot be successful." Pfeffer, Jeffrey, and Robert I. Sutton. *Hard Facts, Dangerous Half-Truths, and Total Nonsense: Profiting from Evidence-Based Management*. Boston, MA: Harvard Business School, 2006. Originally printed in "The Rules of Collaboration," Forbes ASAP, June 5, 1995. p. 88.

should work at something you like, and in an ideal world that makes a lot of sense. But let's face it, if everyone could have the job they liked, there would be no call centres, middle managers, or crime scene cleanup crews.

That's life: opportunity does not always knock on your door with a gift-wrapped package holding the job opportunity of your dreams for you to walk into. There are reasons people are in the jobs they are in—rich or poor, educated or uneducated, qualified or unqualified, first-born or last-born, well-connected family or unknown—either fate, planning, or a little bit of both got you where you are today, and you have to deal with it. To put it bluntly: sometimes shit happens and you need to deal with it the best way you can. A person's job situation may not be ideal, but just because it is not ideal does not mean he should work poorly to demonstrate how unhappy he is in his current situation. He needs to suck it up and be the best he can be. Nobody will hear a worker's sob story and give him the job he wants when his attitude and performance are bad.

Why don't poor performers put as much enthusiasm into their jobs? I understand it is hard for someone to be enthusiastic about a job she cannot do well, but that should not mean she becomes demoralized walking through the door to the office every day. If it does, that shows the character of the poor performer. Is it too much to ask to be positive? You would be surprised what a positive attitude can do to performance, but it appears that in management we focus on motivation and forget about ability and attitude.

Lack of Ability Versus Lacking Specific Skills

In the book *First, Break All the Rules*, there is an example of training in the chapter "How to Manage Around Weakness." One of the examples is about an employee who had the task of turning the author's handwritten notes into PowerPoint presentations.[6] This person was struggling; the quality was poor and the output slowed, which looked like poor performance. However,

---

6   Buckingham, Marcus, and Curt Coffman. *First, Break All the Rules:*

the solution was to provide training. The person assigned to this task had not been taught how to use PowerPoint effectively, but after some appropriate training she become very good at this part of her job.

What sticks out about this example is the task. It is unlikely someone would be hired to do only this task, so it seems likely that this task was given to a junior staff member. The manager states, "She was a brilliant art student, but no one had taught her the detailed mechanics of putting that brilliance onto a computer."[7] Two things stand out here: first, why would the manager think an art student could use PowerPoint, and second, this person was very good at her job otherwise. I think we can chalk up thinking that people learn to use PowerPoint in art school as a flawed assumption—once that mistake had been corrected, this person was able to meet the manager's expectations.

What would the manager have thought if after this training nothing changed for the better? Would the manager put this person on more, or similar, or the same training until she got it? If this person continued to output substandard work in this particular area, would it make sense to terminate her? Of course not; lack of ability in one or two tasks in a given job should not be a reason to terminate. It should be a reason, however, to move some duties around so that important tasks can be completed by those who are competent at them. The overriding theme in this example is that the person in question was competent, just deficient in some technical skills for one particular task. If the person's only job had been to handle PowerPoint slides and she couldn't do that even after the appropriate training, then what?

As I have said earlier, everyone has natural talent, and if a person's talent isn't enough to achieve a manager's expecta-

---

What the World's Greatest Managers Do Differently. New York, NY: Simon & Schuster, 1999. p.164

7   Buckingham, Marcus, and Curt Coffman. *First, Break All the Rules: What the World's Greatest Managers Do Differently*. New York, NY: Simon & Schuster, 1999. p.165.

tion, how is managing that person going to help them achieve the manager's expectation?[8] Instead of identifying this and coming to terms with it, managers provide "special avenues"[9] to try to improve the poor performance so those people can become acceptable in their job. Don't forget that these avenues are devised to help competent employees get back on track to the performance they have been known to reach. Because they are designed to help the competent employee, these programs actually enable poor performance when they are used to try to help a poor performer.[10] How far and how long are managers prepared to go before it becomes completely obvious that everything was an enormous waste of resources? The simple fact is that chronic poor performers are not competent employees, and the tools we use to manage competent employees create a different result when used on poor performers—all because we make the assumption that the chronic poor performer is, was, or can be competent.

---

8   "Given the enduring nature of talent, it is highly unlikely that the person will ever be able to acquire the necessary talent." Buckingham, Marcus, and Curt Coffman. *First, Break All the Rules: What the World's Greatest Managers Do Differently.* New York, NY: Simon & Schuster, 1999. p.167.

9   According to Buckingham and Coffman there are only three possible routes to helping the person succeed "Devise a support system. Find a complementary partner. Or find an alternative role." Buckingham, Marcus, and Curt Coffman. *First, Break All the Rules: What the World's Greatest Managers Do Differently.* New York, NY: Simon & Schuster, 1999. p.168.

10   Enabling responses to poor performance are sympathy/support, job redesign, reassignment, transfer, no action. Parham, Creda Pamler Joe. "The Construct of Substance Abuse Enabling Applied to Poor Performance Management: How Managers Deal with Poor Performing Employees." PhD diss., Virginia Polytechnic Institute and State University, 2003.

The Dunning-Kruger Effect: Unskilled and Unaware of It

Have you ever asked for yourself—I know I have—"What were they thinking?" or "Do they really think they are that good?" Sometimes everything an employee is doing, everything he has produced, is below par in every way, shape, and form, yet he thinks he is doing stellar work. He appears to think he is really contributing in a significant and positive way.

Those in academia recognize this phenomenon and have given it a name: the Dunning-Kruger Effect. The Dunning-Kruger Effect was described in a paper written in 1999 by Justin Kruger and David Dunning titled "Unskilled and unaware of it: How difficulties in recognizing one's own incompetence lead to inflated self-assessments." They stated:

> *People tend to hold overly favorable views of their abilities in many social and intellectual domains. The authors suggest that this overestimation occurs, in part, because people who are unskilled in these domains suffer a dual burden: Not only do these people reach erroneous conclusions and make unfortunate choices, but their incompetence robs them of the metacognitive ability to realize it.*[11]

Their eye-opening study is definitely is worth a read. It has important implications for the problem of poor performance. First, it explains why there is such a significant disconnection between what poor performers think they are producing, and what they are really producing. It also suggests that poor performers may lack the skills to assess and understand feedback

---

11   Kruger, Justin, and David Dunning. "Unskilled and Unaware of It: How Difficulties in Recognizing One's Own Incompetence Lead to Inflated Self-Assessments." *Journal of Personality and Social Psychology*, 77.6 (1999): 1121–1134.

on their performance. The worst-performing study subjects showed poor metacognitive skills. Not only did they not realize that their performance was bad, they didn't change their opinion even after seeing how much better their peers had done. Because poor performers are unable to see the difference between their own poor performance and the good performance of others, they have a limited ability to learn from those around them.

Poorly Defined Expectations: Understanding the Job

Some people out there may say that poor performance is caused by ill-defined objectives: what the manager wants and what the poor performer understands and provides are two different things. I would almost be willing to accept this—except that most people ask questions if they do not understand or are unsure.[12] When objectives are unclear, a good performer sees this, and takes steps to solve the problem. So although properly defined objectives are a necessary part of anyone's ability to perform properly and have someone judge that performance in an objective way, I do not think a lack of well-defined objectives can completely explain poor performance.

You would think performance expectations are pretty clear-cut. The expectation is that workers will do their jobs with the proper level of care and quality for the job and the business. That may be the expectation, but is it ever said? In all the years I have been working, I have never come across someone who outlines what their performance standards are before anyone starts a job. Is that not odd? For something as basic as performing to expectation, one would expect HR or the hiring manager to at least outline what performance level they expect.

---

12   Remember that visceral understanding I spoke of earlier, which seems to be missing with poor performers? How is better defining objectives going to help someone if their metacognitive abilities are lacking or they don't genuinely understand?

I think the reason managers do not say this explicitly is that we expect the employee to inherently know she will meet whatever the performance expectation while performing her job duties.[13] You are probably thinking the job description sets the expectation. In fact, it only sets out the parameters of the job; it usually does not describe the standards to which tasks must be performed in order for performance to be considered good. Even if it did, can we describe performance standards to the point where there is complete understanding and consensus? I do not think so, and this is where we get into metacognitive skills.[14]

Metacognition means "a higher order of knowing." Basically it means knowing whether you know something or not. If a poor performer cannot see his poor performance, which is very possible if he has low metacognitive abilities, carefully describing performance standards will not help because the worker lacks the ability to understand the description.[15] That is a big problem. How can you expect someone to perform to a certain level if he doesn't understand what the performance standards mean and can't assess his performance?

The point here is being self-aware.[16] I find it incredibly hard to believe that if someone can get out of bed and dress herself—

---

13   The closest I came to anyone telling me their performance expectations before the fact was when a history professor said to me at the beginning of the first class, "I expect you to work your ass off." I don't think that can be considered very meaningful since the level of effort was not directly proportional to the mark one would achieve.

14   Meta: "denoting a nature of a higher order or more fundamental kind." Cognitive: "of or pertaining to cognition." Cognition: "the action or faculty of knowing, now spec. including perceiving, conceiving, etc. as opp. to emotion and volition." *New Shorter Oxford English Dictionary.*

15   So much for having a visceral understanding of the term "do a good job."

16   "Knowing own mission, priorities, limits, talent and internal motivation," something it appears the poor performer does not do well. Kosturiak, Jan. "Innovations And Knowledge Management." *Human Systems Management*, 29(1):51–63.

colour-matched to boot—get to work by using a motor vehicle of some sort, get to work at the applicable time, know how to use a computer in the context of her job, find the lunchroom everyday, and support either herself or her family, but still not understand what is expected of her at work, even when it is written down. It boggles my mind.

High performers don't usually have this problem; they are usually self-aware and self-knowing. But for the low performer, who appears to be neither,[17] this raises the question, what is the mandate of a manager? Is it to use every trick in the book to make a poor performer be all he can be[18] or is it to manage the department to make it the most effective department possible? Very good managers get performance out of their staff. They understand what makes their staff tick—how to get them to do more, advance within the organization, and be happy. This skill is lost on staff of the calibre we are talking about: the managers whom you envy have staff who are capable in their jobs, willing to learn and be led, and have potential to be more than they

---

17   According to the authors of "Skilled or Unskilled, but Still Unaware of It: How Perceptions of Difficulty Drive Miscalibration in Relative Comparisons," "higher skilled performers are better judges of their percentile only for easy tasks. For difficult tasks, the opposite is true: The most skilled are the least accurate. Although poor performers account for the bulk of the above-average effect in easy tasks, good performers account for the bulk of the below-average effect in difficult tasks." As a manager, wouldn't you want the difficult tasks to be considered difficult and have people plan accordingly instead of saying they are easy, which seems to be the case with how poor performers perceive things? Burson, K. A., R. P. Larrick, and J. Klayman. "Skilled or Unskilled, but Still Unaware of It: How Perceptions of Difficulty Drive Miscalibration in Relative Comparisons." *Journal of Personality and Social Psychology*, 90(1):60–77.

18   How much can they improve? According to *First, Break All the Rules*, people have a capacity for change, but even they contend it is not that much. The jury is still out as to why, but the reason lies somewhere in the nature versus nurture argument. Buckingham, Marcus, and Curt Coffman. *First, Break All the Rules: What the World's Greatest Managers Do Differently*. New York, NY: Simon & Schuster, 1999. pp. 80–82.

currently are.[19] Poor performers can barely do their jobs, if at all, and cannot advance within the organization. Not only can they not do more than what they're doing, they are generally a drain on resources. This is a major point that most management teaching seems to omit. The underlying assumption seems to be that everyone is competent. What happens when you have a staff member who is lacks the basic skills required for the job and has very little potential to improve, let alone take on a more challenging role? How long are you going to continue to try to get her to improve? At some point someone will ask, "What are you getting in return?" If the answer to that question is, "Not very much," then have not you wasted your time and resources on a project that you knew would fail? Were you deluded into thinking your management skill would help you save this poor soul and somehow make him do more than she was capable of?[20] To me this does not make a whole lot of sense. As managers, we continually assess people's strengths and weaknesses, as well as their potential. It may be couched in different terms, but that is invariably what it is, and if you are doing your job properly, you should have a very good understanding of what people are capable of doing and what they can't do, based on their prior performance.

---

19   "A solidly constructed team affords you the best shot at managing effectively and therefore achieving your goals" Widmann, Nancy C., Elaine J. Eisenman, and Amy Dorn Kopelan. *I Didn't See It Coming: The Only Book You'll Ever Need to Avoid Being Blindsided in Business*. Hoboken, NJ: John Wiley & Sons, 2007. p. 49.

20   As a manager you really have very little control to get your staff to do anything. "You can't make anything happen. All you can do is influence, motivate, berate, or cajole in the hope that most of your people will do what you ask of them." I will also add, if as a manager you have to do backflips to get your staff members to do their job, your staff is not up to the task. Buckingham, Marcus, and Curt Coffman. *First, Break All the Rules: What the World's Greatest Managers Do Differently*. New York, NY: Simon & Schuster, 1999. p. 109.

Unrealistic Expectations: Are You Setting the Bar Too High?

If people are failing you consistently, is it because you are setting the bar too high? Can it be that very few can achieve the expectation that you have set? Are you out of touch with what people can achieve? Do you just refuse to believe that you, the manager, are the problem?

Of course, the poor performer would say the answer to all the above is yes, but what is really the case? There may be situations where your expectations are completely out of touch with reality, and when that happens, you need to listen to your staff and reset your expectations to be more reasonable. If you don't, your demands will cause staff to become belligerent and generally unhappy. If your staff has historically created 20 of something a day, would it makes sense to suddenly demand 35 the next day? Probably not, if nothing has changed. A goal of 23 would push your staff and be more likely in the realm of possibility than 35. Who knows? Maybe in a year, 35 a day would be possible, but over a short time it will be unlikely and cause much grief.

Now, some of you might have picked up on when I said, "if nothing has changed." If the work situation changes, then performance expectations have to change. Maybe it is possible to achieve the same result, but it is not wrong to have the expectation change. For instance, if someone can run 100 metres in 10 seconds downhill, and then requirements were changed to have the same person run 100 metres uphill, the performance expectation should no longer be 10 seconds but something slower. Why? The variables changed, and that means the results will change too. My point is this: you do not create expectations in a vacuum. We base these expectations on information from metrics, company culture, SLAs, or a business need or want. The need or want may be artificial, but for whatever reason someone deems it to be necessary.

One of your jobs as the manager is to ensure that your team

is capable of reaching that standard, whatever it is. If your staff has been languishing in mediocrity or have forgotten what it is like to perform at a high level, then you need to ensure they are capable of reaching the expectations set out. If they can't, the manager needs to change the values of the variables to achieve the expectation. It is like a math equation: if you know that the result is six, then you have to find the values for the variables to make it six. Change shifts, change staffing levels, or change the staff: whatever it takes.

Knowing where to set the bar requires skill and good judgment, but what else can tell you whether you are setting the bar too high? Experience. Time and time again it pops up and puts a situation into perspective because you have been there before. Your experience will tell you what is and is not possible. This is probably a manager's biggest weapon in combating a poor performer's assertions that he cannot complete his tasks, you are expecting too much, or your targets are unreachable. Experience tells us what is possible and what is not. Fortunately, you're a smart person, and you can determine what should be achievable in your particular situation. If some of your staff cannot reach the target you have set, then you have to determine why. More than likely the reason is internal motivation, talent, or skills or a combination of all of these factors,[21] but it will be experience that will tell you that, because it also tells you what people can achieve.

Is your poor performer just someone faced with too high a standard? I would say no. The question of whether expectations are set too high comes into play when no one, or very few workers, can meet expectations. This is not the case if you have people who can exceed the standard and others who can meet it. In a situation like that, you need to look at your individual performers and determine why some can reach the expected standard and others cannot.

---

21   Parham, Creda Pamler Joe. "The Construct of Substance Abuse Enabling Applied to Poor Performance Management: How Managers Deal with Poor Performing Employees." PhD diss., Virginia Polytechnic Institute and State University, 2003.

3

Cost of Poor Performance

Do You Need the Best?

Do You Really Need the Best, or Is Good OK?

This is a question all managers, and their bosses as well, should ask themselves. It is a very important question. Everyone wants top talent—or so they say—but is it entirely necessary? Is it necessary to hire someone who performs better than the rest of the staff? Generally speaking I would say that although I would prefer to have a team of rock stars[1] do the job, the reality is that for most jobs it is not necessary. It's not necessary because for some strange reason things will get done in time as long as the staff is competent.

What I have observed is that everyone is replaceable. When people leave, it takes time to adjust, but everything will eventually return to a state of normalcy. How long does it take? That depends on a host of factors, such as how fast the new party can get up to speed, but during the transition, expectations change as new dynamics set in. What was normal yesterday changes to become what is normal today. Everyone comes to

---

1 Someone who is considered by his peers and by management as the best of the bunch.

accept the new normality because there is really nothing you can or need to do about it.

The TV show *MASH*[2] illustrated this brilliantly. At one point in the series, Radar O'Reilly has received his papers to return home and is training Klinger to replace him. Radar, the company clerk, was also the go-to person for everything needed to maintain the smooth operation of the camp. He ordered supplies, worked the radio, made deals to get contraband, parts, booze, incubators, and anything else the staff of the MASH needed; from all accounts, he was at the top of his game—no one was better. When Klinger, who wears a dress in the hopes of getting a Section Eight discharge, tries to take over from Radar, he is terrible. In the episode "Period of Adjustment" (Season 8, Episode 6), Klinger has spent a couple of weeks learning on the job, but is still not able to be another Radar. Colonel Potter has a conversation with Father Mulcahy about Klinger as the "new Radar" and how woefully inadequate he is. Father Mulcahy tells Potter that when he arrived he had the broken-in model of Radar, the model that could do everything. The implication is that it is unfair to compare Klinger to Radar.

Over time, as Klinger works in his new job, he improves and manages to do everything Radar was capable of doing. It might not be to the level, or speed, from a side-by-side comparison, but it gets done in an acceptable time limit that meets the criteria needed. New expectations create a new norm based on what Klinger can deliver. He eventually becomes competent, but he's never Radar.

So do you need the best? No, you don't need the best. It's nice to have the best, but in the end it is not really necessary as long as the staff you have are competent and intelligent, and most importantly, they are achieving their goals, and not faltering. What does this mean for the poor performer? Although you don't need a rock star, you do need competent people, and a poor performer is not competent. Knowing that you don't

---

2   For anyone who has never seen the show, it is about a group of doctors and nurses in a mobile army hospital unit during the Korean War.

have to have an all-star staff may alter a manager's perspective of what is possible with the allotted staff, but it should not be a reason to lower standards so far that we can include the poor performer in the competent category. If you don't have the best staff, all that should really mean is that your staff have less time to do "value added" work. The "free time" a competent employee has would be less if compared to a high performer doing the same job, so instead of some value added task taking three days to complete for instance, it may now take four or five days. It the grand scheme of things is that really a big deal? If it is, there is always overtime.

Does this mean you should base your expectations on the current abilities of your staff? If so, does it seem likely that the business will ask for what it really wants, or only for what is within the abilities of the staff? There will always be times when deadlines are deadlines and unreasonable demands are necessary. It might be necessary to hire contract staff or for existing staff to work late nights and weekends, but is that demand reasonable? If staff can only do something in three days, does it make sense for management to ask for it to be done in two? Most managers would not ask for two days when they know from experience that three days is the reasonable demand given the abilities of their staff. To get the job done in less time, they would allocate more resources.

If we plan properly, unreasonable demands should be few and far between. Even so, we all know that sometimes everyone needs to scramble to meet a demand. If that task is completed in three days instead of two, how much of a problem would that really be? That depends on the type of business and whether the product is for the public or an internal process. Imagine buying time for an ad during the Super Bowl and only having the commercial ready the day after the Super Bowl? That would be a big problem. But if the task was to have 20 copies of a report photocopied and ready for Wednesday, does it really matter if someone does the job on Tuesday afternoon, Monday afternoon, or even Wednesday morning? It probably doesn't matter as long as the task is complete on the suitable day and time. So we set the expectation and everything seems to go along swimmingly—albeit slower than it could, but as we see that may be just fine. There may be no need to hire a high performer to "pick up the slack" or a manager to "whip her staff into tip-top shape"; average may be just fine for everyone except possibly you, the manager.

Ask yourself why the average performance is making you upset. Maybe you see the potential of what could be, and you are trying to push your staff to see things the way you do. Or maybe you just want things to run tight and smooth because you know what it is like when things are firing on all cylinders. Perhaps you think things are a dismal failure—so inefficient you shake your head every time you walk in the office. But if nobody around you has a problem with the way things are currently running, maybe there really is no problem.

A Person's Ability to Advance: Do We Care? Should We Care?

When we hire people, do we hire them to fill a job vacancy or do we hire them with the hope that they will advance? Once we fill the job vacancy, are we as managers really interested in the new employee's ability to advance, or is his ability to perform the technical aspects of the job paramount? I would say initially it is about filling the job and ensuring the person hired can do the job. No job description I have ever seen says the person hired must have the ability to advance in his career; it usually says there's an "opportunity for advancement." Yet it seems that once we hire a person, we expect them to advance. Why does a company care if an employee wants to advance or can advance within the company?

I think we agree that the ability to provide value added services is desirable in staff. It gives them a breadth of abilities that helps them, and the company in general, in the execution of their daily duties and a lot more. But should a company care whether its staff advances? Yes; it makes sense to keep a good employee in the company. You maintain historical knowledge of the company, which is useful, and there's comfort in the continuity of having long-term staff. If staff members can and want to advance, it is in the best interests of the company to ensure that they can advance within the organization.

If an employee has worked hard and received good performance ratings throughout his career, now what? Is he on the road to a promotion? Does the company really want to promote him? Do we even know whether that person wants to advance? Let's look at this logically. We hired someone to do a job for X amount of money. While in that position, this person demonstrates good or great performance and can do many things, some of them unrelated to his job. He may show leadership capabilities. Now there is a discussion about whether this person is on track for some type of career advancement. I would say that if the person has expressed interest in advancing his career, and the company is willing to spend the time, effort, and money for him to reach their next level, this is a good thing and should be encouraged.

Good employees—the right employees—should be regarded as assets[3] and given the opportunity to achieve more. This benefits them as well as the company, but no one should think this is an altruistic act. The company believes it is gaining an advantage by providing an opportunity for advancement to the right employees. If this is true, what is any company getting out of an employee who can't even achieve an acceptable performance rating, let alone advance? Will these employees ever advance within the company? It's unlikely. Does it make sense for the company to invest in these employees? Probably not, and yet . . . is the company going to provide them a multitude of opportunities to start performing at an acceptable level? We know the answer to this question is a very big yes.

---

3   ". . . people are not your most important asset. The *right* people are." Collins, James C. *Good to Great: Why Some Companies Make the Leap—and Others Don't.* New York, NY: HarperBusiness, 2001. p. 51.

If You Want the Best, Do You Have to Pay for the Best

Have you ever wondered how much thought goes into what HR does when they determine what the salary will be for a specific job? I am sure we have all been through the compensation talk and heard how they arrive at pay bands, levels, salaries, etc. Much work goes into determining those answers, but in the end we get a salary range for a particular job, and our job as a manager is to determine where in that range a person goes.

When a company hires a new person, the company usually offers that person a salary that falls somewhere within a range it deems acceptable. The new employee wants the most she can get, and management wants to pay as little as possible. At some point, there is agreement, and the employee gets a salary that both are comfortable with. That is it in its basic form. But what does this really mean? Usually, management has a limit that they will not exceed and limit they will not go under, so there is already an artificial limit set on the negotiations. This may not be a bad thing, but it does bring up a question or two regarding how we pay for talent.

High performers will not get what they are due, and low performers end up earning more than they should. How do we know this? On day one, we don't know yet what the new employee is worth, unless the manager can go back in time and observe him at his former job. Over time, you see who is doing well, who is not, and who is excelling. Does the manager then step back and say, "I get 20% more work out of two people, I will pay them more than our average performer?" Although it's possible, I have never heard of a company doing that.

In practice, management compensates for talent within a very small range that doesn't accurately reflect a worker's ability to do the job, and this causes morale, attitude, and possibly performance problems. If you have three employees, one poor, the other average, and the other above average, yet the salary difference between the highest- and the lowest-paid is only a few percentage points, how long will it be before people compare their salaries and compare the relative worth of their work with their counterparts?[4] If the difference in salary is small, this may lead to animosity and resentment of the manager for not bringing the compensation more in tune with employee performance. How would a top performer feel if she were only making 2% more than the employee who was performing poorly?[5] How much is enough to make the high performer feel her efforts are being rewarded? The more difficult question is what do you do about the poor performer? The answer regarding the high performer seems obvious: pay her more. But conversely, are you going to have a conversation with the poor performer saying, "We're paying you too much for what we're getting out of you, so to level the playing field we will keep your salary static?"

In an ideal world, you would hold the salary of the poor performer and increase the salaries of the average and high performers. That seems fair, yet I don't know of any company that does this. They let the current standing continue: everyone gets inflation increases, and the company does not really end up paying for talent in the real sense of the word. I am not suggesting that paying in proportion to value received would fix all the ills of the corporate world. Peter Drucker himself said, "There can be no truly simple or truly rational compensation system,"[6] but it would be great if a company said to one of its top per-

---

4   "Compensation . . . always expresses status, both within the enterprise and in society. It entails judgments on a man's worth as much as on his performances. It is emotionally tied to all our ideas of fairness, justice, and equity." Drucker, Peter F. *The Frontiers of Management: Where Tomorrow's Decisions Are Being Shaped Today.* New York: Truman Talley, 1986. p. 299.

5   "How his pay relates to the pay of others, and especially to the pay of the men he considers his peers, is always more important than the absolute amount of his salary . . . It expresses in clear and tangible form a man's position, rank, and recognition within the group" Drucker, Peter F. *The Frontiers of Management: Where Tomorrow's Decisions Are Being Shaped Today.* New York: Truman Talley, 1986. p. 299.

6   Drucker, Peter F. *The Frontiers of Management: Where Tomorrow's Decisions Are Being Shaped Today.* New York: Truman Talley, 1986. p. 298.

formers, "We have looked at your current compensation, and we are increasing it based on your abilities and performance to date to keep in line with our policy of paying for top talent."

Imagine the shift in thinking necessary to do that. Imagine an employee getting pulled into a meeting and being told that? But that is not the real world. The real world is full of inequalities of every type, and performance is just one of them. I guess the question we need to ask is, are performance inequalities really that big a deal? Salaries are very tightly packed with any job; are we to believe the difference in expectations between high and low performers is a matter of degree and that is why companies do not pay their top performers what they should, or is it that they are in an artificial box of acceptable salary levels and cannot see a way to get out of it?

About 25 years ago, the company I worked for had an employee who keyed paper applications into a system. She started at 8:30 am, and she was so fast she finished her quota of applications by noon—and it was quality output. Everyone else finished at the end of the day, and some could not reach their daily quota. Now, the job was not high-paying, but if you are twice as good as the average person, it says to me that you are a rock star, and the company should compensate you more. However, she was already at the maximum salary level for that job, so they could not pay her more.

Shouldn't the company make an exception in a case like this?[7] If they paid her 30%–50% more, she could have worked the full eight-hour day, the company would have kept a stellar employee, and her production would go through the roof. Instead, they told her to complete the quota and after that do some clerical work to fill her time until the end of the day. What purpose did that serve? This just shows how constricted

---

7   "It should be for compensation systems that allow judgment to be used and that enable pay to be fitted to the job of the individual rather than impose one formula on everybody." Drucker, Peter F. *The Frontiers of Management: Where Tomorrow's Decisions Are Being Shaped Today.* New York: Truman Talley, 1986. p. 299.

thinking can be when it comes to compensation. Not wanting to do the clerical work, which was really just designed to keep her busy, she asked if she could leave at noon. Management decided that they couldn't let her leave at noon; instead, they increased her quota of applications to be keyed. The obvious question reared its ugly head: why did she have to do X when others had to do Y for the "same" compensation? Management did not have a good answer to that, so she submitted her resignation. Would it have been reasonable for her to leave at noon? If the same amount of work got done, what was the big deal? The employee would be happy, and productivity would be maintained. As expected, morale tanked after this episode.

This example illustrates what I am trying to say. Companies say they want the best, but when push comes to shove, they won't pay for the best. A company may have a multitude of reasons, but in the end they are mostly artificial. A person is doing job X, at the pay grade of Y; with so much experience plus some good performance ratings, that gets you a salary of Z. Once you have that salary, it is unlikely you will get a real raise excluding inflation raises on a yearly basis. Now, I'm sure some of you are wondering about the following: if we give a worker a higher salary—out of the pay grade for instance— what is to stop him from falling back and doing only minimal work? I am willing to bet the probability of that is very, very low.[8] If that is a concern, how about saying thank you with a bonus every six months, or every quarter—not a bonus determined by some formula, but one based on actual value delivered. If someone is making $30,000 a year but is producing

---

8   This is only the case when " . . . good employees allow conditions to deteriorate through reduction of effort and interest—is likely when HRM inducements and investments are not met with the challenge provided by high levels of expectation—enhancing practices." In other words, if the challenge is there, they will continue to perform well. Shaw, Janson D., Brian R. Dineen, Roulian Fang, and Robert F. Vellella. "Employee-Organization Exchange Relationships, HRM Practices, and Quit Rates of Good and Poor Performers." *Academy of Management Journal*, 52(5): 1016–1033.

30% more than everyone else, why not give him a bonus that reflects that? A $9,000 dollar bonus would be fantastic, especially for someone working in a lower-paying job. I think this is something management should consider: paying for the work done, not just compensating based on a matrix chart and a bunch of formulas. This is simplistic, yes, and fair, for sure . . . and it has zero chance of getting implemented. There are too many variables to consider.

Whatever compensation system you use, keep in mind that people are perceptive, and when they feel they are not getting a fair deal, they will leave.

The Cost of Accommodating Poor Performers

How Poor Performers Affect Team Dynamics

Poor performers waste an astonishing amount of time and money in your company. On top of the obvious loss of productivity, they create tensions and management problems within the team. To use an obvious example, let's say you manage four people making widgets, and the goal is to make a total of 40 a day. John makes fourteen, Susan makes ten, Bob makes ten, but Frank can only make six in the allotted time. Do you pay these people the same amount of money? Logic would dictate that the high performer would make more than the low performer, but you don't want to pay anyone more than the other, so when you notice this discrepancy of output you decree that each member of the team should make ten widgets each day so that you can justify paying each worker the same amount.

John makes ten, Bob and Susan each make ten, but Frank can still only make six for a grand total of 36. You are four short. What do you do? Ask John to make four more? You can do that for a time, but at some point compensation will enter the equation.[9] What about coaching? We try coaching, even though

---

9   "Any compensation system determines a man's place within the group. How his pay relates to the pay of others, and especially to the pay

there has never been an indication that Frank can output ten widgets per day. Meanwhile, John needs to make fourteen while we try to manage Frank to make ten. What if Frank still can't make ten widgets in the allotted time? Are you going to let him start earlier than the rest? Frank needs twelve hours instead of eight to make his ten widgets, and the manager, who has the key to the widget manufacturing facility, has to show up early to let him in or stay late. Is that a reasonable accommodation when the other members of the team are capable of outputting ten widgets in the exact same environment? After some time, the manager will start looking for someone to replace Frank. If, in a team of four, three people can meet the expectation, this tells me the expectation is reasonable, and Frank does not have the skills and talent to do the job.

The ones who cannot reach the standard now will more than likely never be able to, so what do you do? Accommodate them by lowering the standard? This could have some unintended consequences. Hire more staff? Most companies have budgets, so hiring an extra person to pick up the slack neither makes sense nor is an option in most companies. Other staff members will probably have to pick up the slack. This in turn means that you will probably have to manage the staff more closely, and more importantly, you will have to manage the situation. Very soon your team will see this situation for what it is: you are making accommodations.

Poor performance is not a one-time thing; it is a continual thing. Most people are accommodating, and that is the typical nature of any team: team members help each other out because no one can be his best day in and day out. But once you introduce someone who is constantly unable to meet the expected standards, resentment is sure to follow, along with a breakdown

---

of the men he considers his peers, is always more important than the absolute amount of his salary." Drucker, Peter F. *The Frontiers of Management: Where Tomorrow's Decisions Are Being Shaped Today*. New York: Truman Talley, 1986. p. 299.

of team dynamics and grumblings about more money, overtime, time off, etc.

These are all very valid feelings. Your well-oiled machine of a team is now dysfunctional because of a poor performer. This is somewhat linear and idealized way things would end, but the point is when you have an anomaly in your midst you need to deal with it. What does this mean for the team? Will the rock star still be the rock star? Maybe, if you actually have a rock star on the team, but more important it means that the average members of the team all of a sudden have to be not so average. This will do one of two things: either they step up and perform[10] or they falter. If they step up, great, but then there is the whole question of recognition that will invariably come up in one way or another. When the day comes that they feel they are no longer getting a fair deal—whatever that deal is—they will start to look for a new job. By that time they have mentally checked out of the job, and they won't do anything extra[11] for you or the company because in their eyes they already did that and got nothing in return.

If your average performers falter, you have a very serious problem on your hands. No one is performing to your expectation, and your rock star will have to pick up almost all the slack from the other members of the team. It is unlikely that one or two people can carry the entire team and reach the same objectives set out at the beginning of the year, so this means that the team as a whole is not hitting its targets. All the members of

---

10   ". . . Motivated and competent peers will 'take on' some of the role responsibilities in order to help the group meet its goals. In essence, peers compensate for the low performer by intervening and expanding their own roles." Lepine, J. A., and L. Van Dyne. "Peer Responses to Low Performers: An Attributional Model of Helping in the Context of Groups." *Academy of Management Review*, 26(1):67–84.

11   "If management fails to meet an individual's expectations, the individual will refrain from exerting extra effort on behalf of the organization." Andersson, Lynne M., and Thomas, S. Bateman. "Cynicism in the Workplace: Some Causes and Effects." *Journal of Organizational Behavior*, 18:455.

the team may feel they are failing, even though they are working hard. Imagine that—a rock star performing below expectation. What will the conversation be like with that employee? It will not be positive, and it will not be reassuring. You, as the manager, are in big trouble, because this person will leave and then where are you?

You may say this would never happen if the manager were doing her job properly, and you are correct to a certain extent. The manager should have reset priorities and objectives so the staff did not feel as if they were drowning. You have now created unintended consequences. If you cannot change objectives because of this, overtime might be necessary. Is there a budget for that? Someone higher up on the totem pole will wonder why you have to pay staff to work overtime when just a few weeks ago they could get more done without overtime. What if the department you work in is project based? Will the projects miss their deadlines, or will some projects just not get done? I am sure the business will have a thing or two to say about that as well.

Effects That Spread Beyond the Team: How Poor Performers Affect the Company as a Whole

By accommodating a poor performer, what have you created? Monetary cost, business disruption, and a possible shift in team dynamics. How likely are these problems? Depending on the department and what the team does, there may be glaring evidence of things gone wrong or the problems may be very subtle with minimal effects. It is difficult to predict, but all of these outcomes are very possible on some level.

For instance, take the example of a help desk. A poor performer cannot achieve the output required by the SLA, so others need to compensate for him. Remember, it is like a math equation: $A + B + C = D$. If D is a set value and A has changed, B and C have to change to reach D. Failing to meet this SLA might put increased workload on the second-level IT teams. If they are already maxed out, then this will cause performance problems in that team as well, and they might fail to meet their SLA. In the worst-case scenario, it may mean new people are hired into the wrong department because the effects of a problem at a higher level cascaded to the lower levels, where it became more obvious.

Let's say the help desk takes 30 calls a day, and on average refers ten calls to the second level. The second level is staffed according to this demand; we are assuming presently if a second level tech can fix eight of those problems a day that would leave two to be fixed the next day. This means we need two second-level people to ensure all ten incidents are dealt with the same day. Instead of one person handling eight incidents, two people each do five, which is about 63% of their capacity. If things change and we make accommodations so the help desk can now send fifteen tickets a day to second-level techs, the second-level techs will have to work at 100% and 88% of capacity. Here, there is very little room for variances of any sort and burnout, morale, and compensation issues will come up soon.

Let's say for sake of argument that the second level hires another person to compensate for the new load. Now there are three second-level techs, each working to about 63% capacity for incidents related to calls from the help desk. Is the third person necessary? If you look at the workload, the answer is yes. If you look at the reason behind the increase in the workload, the answer is no. The help desk is not reaching its SLA, and the problem cascades to those departments it deals with directly: second-level in this example. We notice the problem in the second level and adjust staffing, but really the staffing issue is at the help desk and we should make the adjustment there.

The company just hired a comparatively expensive person when it could have trained or replaced staff at the help desk to keep the SLA achievable. Looking at the problem with a logical and inquisitive eye to understand why the workload has increased might have showed what the real problem is— training, for instance? If you need to hire staff, make sure you don't hire the wrong staff to fix a symptom of the problem.

There could be many reasons the help desk cannot maintain its service level, and not all of them are attributable to the help desk staff. If things were working within the parameters of the SLA, but now are not, something has obviously changed. Now it is up to you to understand what is breaking down and where the real fix needs to be by looking at the metrics you are collecting and by doing some investigation. Finding the root cause can be difficult and can take time, but it's important to look at the entire process to find the problem, even though it is much easier to throw resources at a problem than to use your brain.

If there is a valid reason staff cannot reach the expected service level, then the expectations needs to be changed. The people affected by the change should be involved because it is not prudent to change an SLA without input from those who agreed to the SLA in the first place. If you do, it can have serious repercussions. Remember: a hiccup or two does not warrant an emergency meeting to determine a new structure for an SLA or a new set of metrics and expectations; it just means you need to watch and see if patterns are emerging. If they are, you need to understand why and act, if necessary.

If you decide to make accommodations, you have to determine for yourself whether those accommodations are necessary, valid, and acceptable because once they are implemented, some very strange things are likely to happen. How will your boss take it when a set of issues arises that you hadn't thought of? You were just trying to do right by your team and give the problem member the benefit of the doubt, but now you look like an idiot.

When you start making expectations relative, you will start having serious problems. Let's say your poor performer is achieving your new lower expectation: how do you handle his yearly performance review? Does he automatically get a lower rating than the others? Say John can only make 20 widgets to Frank's 50 and Susan's 75, so you set the expectation for John to 20. If he manages to pull off 30, should his rating show that he exceeded expectations, or should he be evaluated on the same scale as the others, where it will show that he is still underperforming? Or do you change the objectives of Susan to help John make 50 widgets and then evaluate Susan on John's ability to make 50? If you do that Susan might not exceed her expectations because John cannot meet his. It comes down to this: if Susan's compensation targets are affected by poor performers in some way, she will eventually leave.[12]

From my perspective, it doesn't make sense to make accommodations for a poor performer. What has she done to deserve it? It does not seem logical that never having reached her manager's expectations means that she is given a lower set of expectations to reach.[13] I am sure some management book recommends this approach, but why? A poor performer should never get a bonus or other inducements because, quite simply, giving her a bonus, even a token amount, for not doing their job is wrong. Yet most companies do exactly this. If a worker gets a poor performance rating, but still gets a bonus, what message is that sending? "Your performance is not good, but thanks for the effort. Here is some money anyway." Withholding bonuses may sound heartless, but I don't recall getting a medal for finishing last in a race either.

---

12   This is known as a team-based performance management system. "One particularly problematic area in terms of human resources practises is the degree to which an employee's salary is tied to their team's performance." Kline, Theresa J.B., and Lorne M. Sulsky. "Measurement and Assessment Issues in Performance Appraisal." *Canadian Psychology* 50(3):161–171.

13   As stated previously, this type of behaviour enables poor performance, and "In addition, the over investment exchange relationship (high HRM inducements and investments and low expectation-enhancing practices) may be optimal for poor performers because they receive substantial perquisites without the burden of high expectations." In other words they get the advantage of all the perks of employment and none of the performance expectations that others have to live up to. Shaw, Janson D., Brian R. Dineen, Roulian Fang, and Robert F. Vellella. "Employee-Organization Exchange Relationships, HRM Practices, and Quit Rates of Good and Poor Performers." *Academy of Management Journal*, 52(5):1016–1033.

Think about this for a minute. In the yearly review, the manager states unequivocally that a person has not reached the targets agreed on at the beginning of the year because of his performance. At the end of the meeting, the person receives his performance rating for the year, and it is the equivalent of an F, when the person should be striving for a minimum of C+. Yet this company, which is proud of being a performance-based company with high standards, for instance, provides the poor performer with a yearly bonus. It may be calculated using some formula, which gives the illusion of fairness since the better you perform the more you get, but we all know this graduated scale is flawed and too many times the difference between above average and below average performance is a matter of minor degrees.

Businesses need to stop rewarding poor performance. Not only does it feed the poor performer's delusion of doing well, but it perpetuates her unacceptable behaviour[14]—assuming, of course, there is something she can do about it.

The Dollar Cost of Keeping a Poor Performer

The real question is, how much does it cost to keep a poor performer on board? This is difficult to calculate because there are numerous costs, such as lost opportunity, that we don't have a value for, but we can still make a generalized estimate. Let's assume that each employee earns the same salary, and that the company has a "three strikes and you're out" policy (three chances at improved performance before termination).

The first question we need to ask is, how long does the poor performer work at the job? We also have to determine what we consider poor performance on some numerical scale. With the following scale[15] we can estimate what a poor performer costs

---

14   See Parham, Creda Pamler Joe. "The Construct of Substance Abuse Enabling Applied to Poor Performance Management: How Managers Deal with Poor Performing Employees." PhD diss., Virginia Polytechnic Institute and State University, 2003.

15   This scale is completely subjective, but it allows me to determine in

an organization. Looking at a worker's effort as a percentage of what I think most would consider normal work output we get the following:

1. 30%–45%: Poor performer. Anything less would be a conscious decision not to perform.

2. 46%–55%: Marginal performer. Could potentially become acceptable with work, but only capable of performing at the lower end of the acceptable scale.

3. 56%–70%: Acceptable performer (I personally like 65% as a base for good performance).

4. 71%–100%: High performer. "Rock star" status starts around 80%.

For a person to be worth 100% of his salary, we expect performance of 56%–70%[16] of maximum output. Based on the scale above, a poor performer does approximately 20%–57% less work than a person who we consider an acceptable performer.[17] This discrepancy is large, so let's take a more conservative approach and make the range smaller say, 15%–40%.

What is this going to cost? The cost breaks down as follows:
- work not done by the poor performer,
- time spent by other workers doing the poor performer's reassigned tasks,
- extra time spent by the team manager,
- extra time spent by HR and company management,

---

a numerical way the assessment of someone's performance.

16   "Most people invest about 60 percent of what they are capable of in order to receive a good performance review." Malandro, Loretta A. *Say It Right the First Time*. New York: McGraw-Hill, 2003.

17   "Felps estimates that teams with just one deadbeat, downer, or asshole suffer a performance disadvantage of 30 to 40 per cent." Sutton, Robert I. *Good Boss, Bad Boss: How to Be the Best . . . and Learn from the Worst*. New York: Business Plus, 2010. p. 112.

- time lost by the poor performer in performance evaluations (paid but non-working time).

If we use the timelines three months, six months, one year, and five years as examples, we can at least try to figure out a dollar figure for what this is costing a company. If we assume $100,000 dollars as a salary, and we also assume that a poor performer does 15%–40% less work than an acceptable performer with the same salary we can say that a poor performer costs the company between $15,000 and $40,000 a year.[18]

Broken down by performance level and time spent at the company, we can calculate losses from $3,750 to $300,000:

Salary	$100,000				
less work	15%	40%	45%	50%	60%
Years					
0.25	$3,750.00	$10,000.00	$11,250.00	$12,500.00	$15,000.00
0.5	$7,500.00	$20,000.00	$22,500.00	$25,000.00	$30,000.00
1	$15,000.00	$40,000.00	$45,000.00	$50,000.00	$60,000.00
2	$30,000.00	$80,000.00	$90,000.00	$100,000.00	$120,000.00
3	$45,000.00	$120,000.00	$135,000.00	$150,000.00	$180,000.00
4	$60,000.00	$160,000.00	$180,000.00	$200,000.00	$240,000.00
5	$75,000.00	$200,000.00	$225,000.00	$250,000.00	$300,000.00

---

18   It is impossible to accurately reflect the loss of productivity of knowledge work since it can be very subjective. As well, we are dealing with assumptions and possibilities that may or may not come to fruition. This is not an attempt to show truly accurate numbers, since we cannot know for certain, but it is an illustration of the potential monetary loss in relation to the work level provided.

This is just in lost productivity for the poor performer. If we include productivity lost by all the other workers dealing with the poor performance of one person, we are looking at additional productivity losses over a year:

1. HR: over the course of a year I do not think 12 hours is an unreasonable estimate. That is one hour every month.

2. Manager: 30 minutes a week for 52 weeks to try to keep the poor performer on track: 26 hours.

3. Manager's manager: keeping the manager apprised of the situation. Twelve hours for the year.

4. Staff: someone's time compensating for the lack of performance within the group, potentially to the tune of $15,000–$60,000 a year.

5. Overtime: if applicable, let's assume 1 hour extra a day for a year, which comes to about $11,520 a year.

The final total is 50 hours of lost productivity for all people involved, which, at $48/hour, comes to $2,400 from other staff, i.e., HR etc. If we include overtime of $11,520, we have a total of $13,900 to compensate for a poor performer. On top of the original lack of productivity, we can now calculate costs from $7,225 to $578,000.

% less work	15%	40%	45%	50%	60%
Years					
0.25	$7,225.00	$19,266.67	$21,675.00	$24,083.33	$28,900.00
0.5	$14,450.00	$38,533.33	$43,350.00	$48,166.67	$57,800.00
1	$28,900.00	$77,066.67	$86,700.00	$96,333.34	$115,600.00

% less work	15%	40%	45%	50%	60%
2	$57,800.00	$154,133.34	$173,400.00	$192,666.67	$231,200.00
3	$86,700.00	$231,200.00	$260,100.00	$289,000.01	$346,800.01
4	$115,600.00	$308,266.67	$346,800.01	$385,333.34	$462,400.01
5	$144,500.00	$385,333.34	$433,500.01	$481,666.68	$578,000.01

The $100,000 dollar salary we used for this illustration has now climbed to $193,000 for the total yearly cost of a poor performer who underperforms by 50%. That is a 93% increase of his salary to manage him and attempt to maintain productivity within the department. Even if we agree that we were too liberal with our estimate and cut it in half, we are still in the realm of 45%, which still borders on the unbelievable.

If we include the cost of training to help a poor performer get back on track, we are looking at probably $3,000 dollars for a 5-day course. Five days of not working equals $1,923 dollars, so there is another figure to be added to the never-ending amount of money these poor performers are costing the company. If we have to hire contract staff to help with the workload, we are looking at substantially more than $13,900. We could be looking at a full salary for potentially a year, even if we use a more conservative salary like $50,000 dollars, you can see the cost is still overwhelming.

Considered another way, your poor performer is losing between 1 and 3 hours of expected productivity daily. On the extreme side of the scale, she could potentially be losing 5 hours a day. Ouch! How many organizations, departments, or managers can afford to have any staff member with that level of productivity? I doubt any, yet the prevailing thinking is these people are capable and willing and because of that assumption their level of productivity is tolerated while they attempt to improve to the point of acceptability. If managers are spending time and effort on improving one person so she can make the grade, isn't it an entirely more productive use of time and money to use those resources on someone who is already making the grade and *wants* to achieve more? From my perspective the answer is yes.

At this point, we have not even touched on the cost of loss of reputation, dropped projects, or lost opportunities—if it is even possible to put a dollar figure on those things. I think you are starting to get the point. Poor performers cost the company substantially more money than they are worth.

4

What Can You Do?

How Conventional Management Strategies Fail to Deal Effectively with Poor Performance

Can a Poor Performer Improve?

Sometimes employees are simply working below their ability. People who were working below their ability but are now reaching their potential are not so much displaying the Hawthorne effect, a phenomenon whereby people change their behaviour as a result of being watched, they weren't applying themselves before because they could afford not to. When people choose not to work to their potential, it is the fault of the organization as a whole. Some organizations demand greatness but do nothing to achieve that goal except to spout empty words about being a performance-based company. When mediocrity pervades the organization, it makes little sense to try to be better because there is no benefit. You could try, but the level of inertia to be overcome would be too great to make any meaningful difference.

For workers who are coasting, measuring their performance

with metrics can provide some incentive: who wants to get into trouble because of his performance? When they kick their performance up a notch, this shows management that those people are capable of more; they just need an environment that expects and rewards high performance.[19] Either way, people are coasting because management is not doing its job. The job of a manager is get her staff to perform at or above expectation.

In contrast, no amount of coddling, yelling, incentives, or tricks will make a poor performer good. Because external motivation is weak, we have no control even over people who are competent, let alone over a poor performer. This needs to be acknowledged because if it is not, managers will fall into the trap of continually trying to improve someone who is not capable of improving. This is as counter-productive as giving a medication for a condition even when several attempts have shown it does not work. Instead of stopping and trying something different, you continue to administer the medication in the hopes that it will eventually start working.

Can a poor performer improve? Anyone can improve, but how much? Can a poor performer bring his performance to an acceptable level? For example, is a 5% improvement enough? If it is, then the poor performer is not a true poor performer. If he improves 5% but needs to improve 30%, then he still fails to reach acceptable performance. You may think 30% improvement is a little too much to expect, and I agree. This is where a person's natural ability comes into play. Natural ability is the reason some people can reach the goals you set, but others

---

19   In 1982, GM closed a plant. It was reopened by Toyota in 1985 to form New United Motor Manufacturing. They hired 85% of the staff from the old plant, and with training and a better environment it became one of the best plants for the highest quality and lowest cost. Pfeffer, Jeffrey, and Robert I. Sutton. *Hard Facts, Dangerous Half-Truths, and Total Nonsense: Profiting from Evidence-Based Management.* Boston, MA: Harvard Business School, 2006. p. 40. Originally printed in "The Rules of Collaboration," Forbes ASAP, June 5, 1995, p. 98. Originally in Charles O'Reilly III and Jeffrey Pfeffer. *Hidden Value.* Boston, MA: Harvard Business School Press, 2000.

cannot, and poor performers don't have the natural ability to achieve good performance.

Do the other workers cheat or somehow skew their results to make themselves look better than they really are? Remember, metrics—cold, hard facts—can show you the true difference between your best, average, and worst. Some people do the same jobs in various companies, with the same tools, yet some are better than others. If the standard you set is 100 and your poor performer is at 70 or below, your average person is at 100, and your best is at 120, it is obvious that people can achieve the standard. Given the talent they have been born with and all the knowledge, training, and skills they have achieved over a lifetime, can poor performers reach 100? I would almost guarantee that they cannot. You are left to decide whether to lower the bar to accommodate them.

Management Versus Supervision: Is One Better than the Other?

Do you distinguish between managing[1] and supervising[2] someone? Most people think these are one and the same, but in dealing with a poor performer there is a massive difference. Supervising means getting people to do something a certain way, whereas management means being responsible for the end result.

I can explain this best through the following illustration: You have been charged with the task of installing new grass in a backyard. Your staff consists of workers and a supervisor, and you are the manager. People have their own particular tasks, and to ensure that you cannot get too intimately involved (by micromanaging), you sit on the top rung of a ladder that overlooks the backyard. The supervisor can walk anywhere, and the

---

1   Managing: "That manages; (a) having executive control or authority." *New Shorter Oxford English Dictionary.*

2   Supervise: "oversee the actions of work (a person)." *New Shorter Oxford English Dictionary.*

workers can all perform the tasks necessary to get the job done. The manager defines what the backyard is, what is necessary, what completion looks like, and the timeline for the job. More than likely, this job is part of a bigger whole that the manager is responsible for.

Once we define the parameters of the job, it is up to the supervisor to make sure that the workers get the job done to the right level of quality. The supervisor gives out the job assignments, and tells the workers what needs to happen and in what order. The workers complete the tasks in the necessary time and with due care and quality. The supervisor monitors their work and the pace and reports to the manager whether things are on track or not. With that information, the manager hires more resources, buys more supplies, or modifies the objective based on the information provided by the supervisor, if applicable. If everything goes according to plan, nothing should really happen other than the completion of the tasks in the specified time and quality.

Remember, the manager is sitting on the ladder; he can see what is happening but cannot make out the minute details. He makes decisions based on the information from his supervisor. A director is sitting higher than the manager, say in the house. She can see even less detail, but gets the general gist of what is happening based on her observations and information provided by the manager. The director will not concern herself with the individual tasks. She only makes sure that the project is on track and on budget, because she is looking at a bigger picture than the manager.

This system falls apart if a poor performer starts reporting to a manager. A manager should be telling his staff what needs to be done, not how to do those things.[3] He will provide a direction with some parameters of what needs to happen, expecting that the staff will figure out what needs to be done

3   Buckingham, Marcus, and Curt Coffman. *First, Break All the Rules: What the World's Greatest Managers Do Differently.* New York, NY: Simon & Schuster, 1999. pp. 110–111.

and how. Poor performers cannot really get a handle on this. They start to thrash about, worrying about minute details that have no bearing on the issue at hand. Their concept of what is important is skewed, and because of this, they end up shuffling when they should be leaping forward. When it is too late, poor performers, overwhelmed by the complexity of what they need to do, do nothing and fail the objective.[4]

Being Closely Managed

Should a manager be monitoring someone's progress closely? No: that is the job of the supervisor. If a poor performer were having problems with something, the supervisor would stand over her and ensure that she completes the task correctly and within the proper time. Is this a good use of the supervisor's time? Probably not, and this approach also has the drawback of not giving your staff an opportunity to grow and become the independent workers you want so you can stop supervising.[5] However, you need to supervise closely when you have a poor performer in your team. Surely some of you are saying, "Hey, I don't have a supervisor, but I need to be on top of my people all the time to make sure I get what I want." If that is the case, you should ask yourself, "Do I need better people?" Having better people would mean not having to stand over your staff. You could actually manage instead of supervise.

Unfortunately, the poor performer will always need some form of oversight. And how much does that cost?[6] As we have

---

4   "Defining the right outcomes does expect a lot of employees, but there is probably no better way to nurture self-awareness and self-reliance in your people." Buckingham, Marcus, and Curt Coffman. *First, Break All the Rules: What the World's Greatest Managers Do Differently*. New York, NY: Simon & Schuster, 1999. pp. 110–111.

5   Buckingham, Marcus, and Curt Coffman. *First, Break All the Rules: What the World's Greatest Managers Do Differently*. New York, NY: Simon & Schuster, 1999. pp. 110–111.

6   "Felps estimates that teams with just one deadbeat, downer, or asshole suffer a performance disadvantage of 30 to 40 per cent." Sutton, Robert

shown earlier, a poor performer creates 1–3 hours of work a week for his peers or manager just to check his work. That may not sound like much, but over a year that is 40–120 hours: 1–3 weeks of checking someone's work. Hard to believe, right?

Will You Let Them Work Independently?

With good or great employees, you have confidence that whatever they do will be fine. We have all known people like that: it did not matter if it were to relay a message, get something from someone, or provide you with something on a given date—if you involved them, you knew it would get done. How much confidence do you have in your poor performers? I don't have any. I have come to terms with it. This is what allows me to sleep at night. It comes down to trust[7]—either you trust your people or you don't. Can you rely on people you do not trust? Maybe for something minor, but mostly no. There is a reason you cannot trust them, and that reason is their past performance and your past experiences with them. Can you really afford to let them work independently if you do not trust them? Probably not: it's a good bet that the work will either be late, or of substandard quality.

If a deadline is important, then as a manager you have a choice: either you do the work yourself, (very bad, but sometimes necessary), heavily supervise a poor performer[8] (a degree or two better than the first option, but a waste of resources), or give it to someone you know will give you what you want

---

I. *Good Boss, Bad Boss: How to Be the Best . . . and Learn from the Worst.* New York: Business Plus, 2010. p. 112.

7   Trust: "faith or confidence in the loyalty, strength, veracity, etc. of a person or thing." *New Shorter Oxford English Dictionary.*

8   "The moment you feel the need to tightly manage someone, you've made a hiring mistake. The best people don't need to be managed. Guided, taught, led—yes. But not tightly managed." Collins, James C. *Good to Great: Why Some Companies Make the Leap—and Others Don't.* New York, NY: HarperBusiness, 2001. p. 56.

in the allotted time (most efficient). My money is on the latter, not just because it is the most efficient but also because it makes the most sense. Would you give the ball to the player with the worst scoring record with only five seconds left in the game and the score tied? No, you would give it to your best shooter, the person who has consistently shown he has the skills to pull it off. Why do we think business is different when it really is not?

Setting SMART Objectives

Setting objectives is at the root of determining whether something has been accomplished; however, we must remember that it is essential to set objectives that make sense. If I said, "We are driving to Florida and will arrive tomorrow," is that an objective? Some would say yes, but it needs more detail. Arriving the next day at 11:59 pm is technically the same day, but I am sure no one would agree with you that you arrived tomorrow. To help prevent those types of situations and ensure that objectives are specific and meaningful, we should create objectives that are SMART. What does it mean? SMART is an acronym:

- S—Specific
- M—Measurable
- A—Achievable
- R—Relevant
- T—Time-bound

I have seen many people get burned on their performance assessments because they did not understand their objectives, or their manager did not know how to create SMART objectives. All people like to succeed, and some like to take the most difficult assignments and make them their own. That is great, but you cannot measure success properly unless there are some parameters. Remember, someone other than yourself will determine whether an objective was met. If we want to succeed as managers, we need our staff to succeed, and we do that by giving them, or getting our staff to create, specific, measurable, achievable, relevant, and time-bound objectives. That is why they are SMART. Does it make sense to present some nebulous idea with ill-defined variables or vague parameters as an objective and expect someone to actually achieve that goal?

A perfect example is right out of the movie *The Lord of the Rings*. Sauron says to Saruman, "Build me an army worthy of Mordor."

This is a nebulous objective. It leaves too much room for interpretation and has no time component to work against. I am sure Sauron thought it was clear what he meant—he said "worthy of Mordor" after all—but that is still vague, unless that saying has a very specific meaning, which I doubt. All this really does is set the expectation that the army needs to be very, very good. Now, we also know that Saruman is probably a high performer—he is a white wizard for God's sake—and since he is dealing with a psychotic it is probably in his best interests to overbuild and not ask too many questions. However, if we were to make a SMART objective out of the directive, "build me an army worthy of Mordor," Sauron should have said something like this: "Build me an army of 10,000 Uruk-hai warriors with body armour, helmets, and weapons, in three months so they are ready and able to attack Helm's Deep."

Let's break this down so you can see the various parts:

S—Specific: Build me an army of 10,000 Uruk-hai warriors, outfitted with body armour, helmets, and weapons. I could be more specific about the type of armour and weapons, i.e., a sword 24 inches long, sharp on both sides, weighing six pounds, etc. You can consider these requirements to be the SMART objectives for those responsible for making the swords. This works into the main objective of building an army worthy of Mordor.

M—Measurable: Did you give Sauron 10,000 Uruk-hai warriors? Did you provide amour, helmets, and weapons for each? Were you able to provide these in the allotted time? These are the measurable components that will be assessed when the time limit for the objective expires.

A—Achievable: Is it possible to make 10,000 Uruk-hai with all the fixings in three months? There would have to be a few discussions to determine the feasibility of making this happen. Saruman can raise concerns here. Maybe there was a discussion between Saruman and Sauron in which Sauron said he wanted the army built in three weeks, and Saruman came back and said, "Impossible. Here are the reasons: x, y, z." After a lengthy discussion, they could have agreed that three months was possible. Once you agree, you are saying the objective is achievable.

T—Time: In three months. This is a time component. An objective must have a time limit, otherwise what is the point? Imagine if the minions of Saruman took 36 months to build that army? Not only would the whole point of the army be lost, but with no time limit, the success of the objective could never be measured.

So if we translate that to business, you have an objective and a set of related tasks necessary to achieve that objective. This is not rocket science, but many people are faced with nebulous objectives every day without understanding that if you are responsible for something, you'd better make damn sure you know what success looks like, because if success is ill defined you are setting yourself up for failure. Even the rock star of the team will more than likely fail to meet objectives that are too vague or improperly defined.

How does this relate to poor performers? SMART objectives are a two-way street. If someone has a SMART objective, it is easy for a manager to determine whether the worker is on track to meet that objective. This, depending on how you look at it, may or may not be a good thing. With SMART objectives, there is nowhere to hide. In the example above, if you do not make 10,000 Uruk-hai, you have failed. If you do not provide armour, helmets, and weapons, you failed. If you cannot do it in three months, you failed. If they cannot attack Helm's Deep, you failed.

The more nebulous goal of "build me an army worthy of Mordor" could mean 50 people, each armed with a club, slingshot, and a bad attitude. It would be substantially more difficult to say you did not achieve the objective when technically you did what you understood[9] and that was build an army. Poor performers typically live in the nebulous world, not really venturing out into the SMART world because it is just too difficult and shines a glaring light on their inadequacies as an employee when measured against others. A poor performer seldom thinks out her objectives very well, and she usually does not include the SMART criteria. Poor performers also tend to be somewhat grandiose, which results in objectives that are huge but not very well-defined. No wonder there is a disconnect between them and their managers!

When it comes to objectives, the manager has a very large role to play. It is his responsibility to ensure that the objectives of his staff are SMART. Unfortunately, there are managers who have not gotten this concept yet, and they can be one of the chief contributors to their staff not achieving their goals. Every manager needs to make sure his staff have SMART objectives. If they don't, the manager and staff need to go back to the drawing board and make those objectives SMART. It is for the good of both staff and management, because when staff miss their objectives, the manager invariably will also miss some component of his objectives, and the dominoes will fall in succession. SMART objectives help to prevent that type of issue as much as possible. If an objective is not on track, either you or your staff can take corrective measures to get it back on track. If you can't get back on track, then at least you can tell your boss why and modify your plans and objectives accordingly. Setting

---

9   Remember visceral understanding? I know an army isn't 50 people, based on the context of Middle Earth, but I also know an army needs weapons. If it were me I would ask a few questions. Even if Saruman were vague in answering them, you could come to a better conclusion by asking some clarifying questions.

objectives is all about managing expectations—something poor performers do not do very well.

Always and only create objectives that you can control. The reason is this: if you rely on another department or organization for something you need in order to complete your objective, you run the risk of that objective being unrealized. This happens for the very simple reason that your priorities are not the same priorities of others. If a time constraint or some other resource constraint appears, you can be quite sure your objectives will not be someone else's highest priority. I am not talking about projects where assigned resources ensure project completion; I am talking about tasks related to an objective.

For example, you might ask someone to help you create macros for an Excel spreadsheet. Another example is if another department is implementing a new system in your office, and you ask for your department to be included. You eagerly put this new system implementation on your objectives, even though they are doing all the work and you have nothing to do with actually putting it in place. During the year, the department responsible for the implementation changes its priorities, and now you are in trouble because you have an objective that you have no control over. This is a critical error in judgment. You have now failed to meet a large portion of your objectives because of someone else's actions. That does not sound like a good reason to fail, does it?

Is Managerial Motivation Effective?

People have to be responsible for their own motivation. I firmly believe that. No amount of external motivation will get you to do something for long. In the context of your job, you have to want to do the job and do it well. Let's take an in-depth look at motivation, specifically internal motivation, and how it fails to play a part in a poor performer's repertoire of motivational stimuli.

External Motivation

What gets you out of bed in the morning? Money? Sure, I would agree with that, but let's take a closer look. What if you got two cents every time you woke up at 4:30 am when your normal waking time is 9:00 am? That wouldn't motivate me, and I am pretty sure it wouldn't motivate you either. What if it was $10,000 every time you woke up at 4:30 am? I would do it. I am sure many others would do it too, but at some point the desire for the extra four and a half hours of sleep would override the greed factor, and you would say, "I have enough money" and sleep in.

Money is an example of an external motivation. External motivation is the one everyone understands because it is tangible. Motivations can be positive or negative. "Testify against the mob boss and I will kill your family!" Are you going to testify? Probably not—unless you don't like your family. External motivation must offer something that the person perceives as a benefit in some way. In the examples just described, the benefit is keeping your family alive or receiving $10,000.

In business, we can only motivate staff externally. How do we do that? External motivation comes in two broad categories: positive and negative, or the carrot and the stick. Here is a list of examples:

Positive	**Negative**
• Money	• Reprimand
• Challenge	• Humiliation
• Opportunity	• Embarrassment
• Reward	• Punishment
• Recognition	
• Award	

As you look at this very small list, you will identify with at least some of them, and you will probably find you have used some of them as well. Positive motivations should elevate your employees to do what they need to do, whereas negative motivations are essentially coercion—do it or else! With negative motivation you definitely do not get buy-in from your staff, but sometimes it is necessary depending on the situation. Essentially, negative motivation is a pain point that gets stimulated in the hope that a particular staff member will comply with the request and do it to the satisfaction of the requestor. When staff do not perform and you use a negative motivational technique to get them to perform, how do you think they will react? It is somewhat of a vicious circle. The staff does not perform, so you give them a deadline with some coercion put in for good measure. The staff does not meet the deadline, so you reprimand them and start to micromanage or heavily supervise them. Now morale drops and working habits become worse. You reprimand them again for their lack of commitment, and the next thing you know, performance is spiralling downward for the whole group.[10]

This situation of being set up to fail only applies to competent employees who are now categorized as poor performers because of the manager's behaviour (the employee also has a part to play in this). The reason I bring it up is to show that poor performance can be created by a manager. If you find yourself inheriting a team or an employee who is now performing poorly, you need to understand what the team dynamics were before you got there. If you are the problem, you need to understand that instead of pointing fingers and labelling staff as poor performers. A quick litmus test is to ask what has changed. If your staff were doing good work before, but are now beginning to falter under your direction, what variable has changed? It's difficult for anyone to admit she is the problem, but everyone needs to realize that sometimes the problem she is looking for is staring at her from the bathroom mirror.

Unlike most people, I make a distinction between a true poor performer (a.k.a. chronic poor performer) and a pseudo-

10   For greater insight into this very real problem, read Manzoni, J. F., and Jean-Louis Barsoux. *The Set-Up-To-Fail Syndrome: How Good Managers Cause Great People to Fail.* Boston, MA: Harvard Business School, 2002.

poor performer. A pseudo–poor performer is what I call someone who is competent in his current position, but for various reasons cannot reach his manager's expectation. These reasons are usually external, and once the reasons are dealt with, performance improves to its usual level. Poor performance for these people is transient and not the norm, so helping them through a rough patch by modifying their workload or changing expectations makes sense. This is not the case with a chronic poor performer, who consistently performs below expectation.

Once a manager determines that the set up to fail syndrome does not apply in this case and she truly has a chronic poor performer, how can the manager motivate her employee to start performing better? It is obvious that negative motivation does not have a lasting effect or even work in most cases, so why not see how positive motivation will work on a chronic poor performer?

Using Positive Motivation with the Poor Performer

To set the scene, imagine an employee who has continually been failing to meet his objectives—in fact, he might not have been able to meet his manager's expectations from day one. Instead of giving him some type of negative motivation, we are going to see what positive motivation does. Which of the positive motivations should we start with? Money? Really? I do not think offering an employee more money to do his job when he has not met the expectations set out in his objectives makes sense.[11] If it did, everyone would want to be a poor employee, which would create an utter mess.[12] If not money, then a promo-

---

11   "Merit raises are always introduced as rewards for exceptional performance." Even if it is decided this is not what it is, everyone will understand it as such. Drucker, Peter F. *The Frontiers of Management: Where Tomorrow's Decisions Are Being Shaped Today.* New York: Truman Talley, 1986. p. 170.

12   "There is no more powerful disincentive, no more effective bar to motivation, than dissatisfaction over one's own pay compared to that of one's peers." Drucker, Peter F. *The Frontiers of Management: Where Tomorrow's Decisions Are Being Shaped Today.* New York: Truman Talley, 1986. p. 170.

tion? Why would we give a poor performer a promotion for not doing his job? Promoting poor performers to ensure they do their job is not the right reason, and it will also foster poor performance among others if the reward of doing so is a promotion.[13]

Opportunity sounds promising, but should we give someone an opportunity to do something else if she has not shown she can do her job currently? Maybe some of your staff are in the wrong position, but that does not mean they should get a free pass to do something else because they cannot do their current job. If staff want to move to another position, they should show that they can work well and not complain about their lack of opportunity to showcase their skills. A person's performance and attitude are an indication of how she will most likely perform in another job. Every manager says in some way, "Show me what you can do." If that is the question, how can a manager honestly give a poor performer a new opportunity when the worker has never shown that she would be able to excel, meet expectations, or be able to do the job?

One thing is clear in every workplace: people are hired to do a job, whatever that job is. I have never heard of a case where someone goes to a job interview and, after jumping through the various hoops to get hired, becomes an employee without a specific job.[14]

The book *First, Break All the Rules* is rife with examples regarding weaknesses and non-talents. Great managers say, "There are only three possible routes to helping a person succeed. Devise a support system. Find a complimentary

13   This flies in the face of the well-known Peter Principle, which is promoting someone to their level of incompetence, not promoting someone to a second level of incompetence. Peter, Laurence J., and Raymond Hull. *The Peter Principle*. New York: W. Morrow, 1969.

14   Wells Fargo can be considered the exception. "They hired outstanding people whenever and wherever they found them, often without any specific job in mind." Collins, James C. *Good to Great: Why Some Companies Make the Leap—and Others Don't*. New York, NY: HarperBusiness, 2001. p. 42.

partner. Or find an alternative role."[15] However, in each of the examples they use the people are considered exceptional. They are "superbly productive," "brilliant," or "very talented."[16] No manager has ever used those words for a poor performer.

Recognition and rewards seem to make some sense as positive motivational carrots to offer someone who is failing at his job, but what this is really doing is lowering the bar on performance. This will send mixed messages, and ultimately the poor performer thinks he is doing a good job[17] when really he is not up to the task. It will be very hard for the worker receiving this recognition to understand or accept any criticism of his work and abilities if he is receiving recognition.

Instead of recognition it may make the most sense to offer some positive feedback. But the positive feedback is only necessary because the person cannot do the job to begin with so, what is it we are recognizing exactly? Great effort? How is it a great effort if the person is currently not meeting the expectations of the manager for her objectives or tasks? How can we consider the person to be doing a great job, or even a good job when it really is not the case? I suppose we can recognize that the person may be working hard to reach expectations, but is it

---

15   Buckingham, Marcus, and Curt Coffman. *First, Break All the Rules: What the World's Greatest Managers Do Differently.* New York, NY: Simon & Schuster, 1999. pp. 167–178.

16   One exception was their example that relates to a person who by the definition we are talking about may be considered a poor performer (she could not count), but since it was a policy of the company to hire mentally challenged employees, we cannot expect the same rules to apply in cases like these. Buckingham, Marcus, and Curt Coffman. *First, Break All the Rules: What the World's Greatest Managers Do Differently.* New York, NY: Simon & Schuster, 1999. pp. 167–178.

17   "Human beings will behave as they are being rewarded—whether the reward is money and promotion, a medal, the autographed picture of the boss, or a pat on the back." Drucker, Peter F. *The Frontiers of Management: Where Tomorrow's Decisions Are Being Shaped Today.* New York: Truman Talley, 1986. p. 299.

really fair to anyone to reward someone's hard work when all that hard work still causes a failure to meet expectations? This has to do with relative and absolute performance perceptions. On an absolute level the poor performer may marginally improve, but on a relative level he still has not reached the requisite standard. It seems that the tasks or objectives set out are too difficult for some people and if they cannot reach the requisite standard, they likely will not receive encouragement, but rather questions about why they cannot meet the challenge,[18] especially if in the same group of people there are those who can meet or exceed the expectation. After you find the answers to these types of questions, are you going to make accommodations? Remember that if you do there could be unintended consequences.

We've now considered money, opportunity, and recognition as possible ways to positively motivate the poor performer. The problem with all of these approaches is that it doesn't make sense to reward someone when she has not done anything of substance to deserve it. A reward says thank you for doing a good job, usually after something has been completed. We do not design a reward to encourage a poor performer to continue trying to do better. Rewarding someone on this basis creates a slippery slope to entitlement. There will come a time when everyone will come to expect rewards not because they deserve them but because they now believe it is their right to receive them.[19]

---

18 "How someone follows up on a failed objective will depend on whether they feel the reason for the failure is internal or external based on past experiences with the particular employee." Latham, G. P., L. L. Cummings, and T. R. Mitchell. "Behavioral Strategies to Improve Productivity." *Organizational Dynamics*, 9(3):4–23.

19 "Economic incentives are becoming rights rather than rewards. Merit raises are always introduced as rewards for exceptional performance. In no time at all they become a right. To deny a merit raise or to grant only a small one becomes punishment." Drucker, Peter F. *The Frontiers of Management: Where Tomorrow's Decisions Are Being Shaped Today.* New York: Truman Talley, 1986. p. 299.

When we reward poor performance, we create an undesirable conditioned response. To elicit the "proper" behaviour from staff, we believe that when they perform well, they must receive some sort of external motivation in order to keep performing well. This is fine in theory, but when someone is being rewarded for inadequate performance, even if he is attempting to improve his performance, it alters the playing field in a negative way. Once this road has been travelled, management will have a very hard time changing the new thinking that will show up.[20] When you try to reset the expectation of rewards, people will see management as a bunch of tyrants and convince themselves that they are victims. Comments such as "I can't believe I have to do that now!" or, "Oh my God, how do they expect anyone to do that?" will soon follow. People may not say these things to a manager's face, but if management has been rewarding poor performance, this is how some staff will receive any request for normal performance.

How about recognizing that some people's best is not good enough and telling them that they are not performing well enough? I think that is more humane than praising them for the illusion of better performance when it is obvious they cannot meet their manager's expectations. If a worker cannot meet the expectation,[21] she should know she cannot do it, and you as the manager should also know and make the proper decisions so that the job can get done.

---

20   "Extrinsic rewards are easy to give and are powerful short-term motivators. The drawback is that they become addictive. Once you are motivated by an external reward for an action, you expect it the next time you perform the same action. And worse, as the novelty wears off, you may begin to expect more for the same amount of effort." Kim, Sang H. *1,001 Ways to Motivate Yourself and Others.* Turtle Press, 1996. p. 13.

21   "For every minute you allow a person to continue holding a seat on the bus when you know that person will not make it in the end, you're stealing a portion of his life, time that he could spend finding a better place where he could flourish." Collins, James C. *Good to Great: Why Some Companies Make the Leap—and Others Don't.* New York, NY: HarperBusiness, 2001. p. 56.

In the end, it appears that external positive motivation is not effective[22] in helping a poor performer improve his performance. We have seen that there are too many negative outcomes, and as well, I find the logic strange: As an employee, I will do my job but you need to give me X, Y, and Z. If I do not get those things I will become unmotivated and end up working poorly. I am not saying that getting extra from an employer is a bad thing, but are an employee's development and happiness in the workplace conditional on the things they get from the employer? We are talking about people here, and it is naïve to think that giving someone a bonus or basketball tickets, or sending him to five courses this year instead of two will keep him "loyal" and happy indefinitely.

If external positive motivation will not help the situation, your other option is to use some negative motivation. As I have said earlier, negative motivations are about coercion: do it or else. But how do you really think those motivations are going to fare in the grand scheme of things?

Internal Motivation

How about internal motivation? Internal motivation comes from within, from being a part of who you are. It is the drive that gets you up when you don't want to, and the drive that makes you try again and again when logic says you should stop. It is difficult to put a finger on it exactly because it is internal, but it is extremely important. Without internal motivation, 99% of the things you accomplished in your life would not have happened.

This is where I find things get a little dicey. From what I have seen, poor performers have a much different level or type of internal motivation than high performers. Some would say it is a defeatist attitude, and I have seen many poor performers

---

22   ". . . you will not need to spend time and energy 'motivating' people. If you have the right people on the bus, they will be self motivated." Collins, James C. *Good to Great: Why Some Companies Make the Leap—and Others Don't.* New York, NY: HarperBusiness, 2001. p. 74.

who have this, but I think it goes further. Having little internal motivation does not mean that everything you do will fail; it depends on the expectation. But there does seem to be a disconnection between a poor performer's ability and her desire to perform well. Most people I know who have trouble with something want to change that, and they find a way to make it happen. Poor performers seem to lack this essential ingredient that tells them to get in gear and become better. It is almost as if they can't improve because their mind somehow tells them that they can only be as good as they are. Their potential for improvement is not very high, nor is their out-of-the-box talent or skill, and it shows in their ability. There must be a relationship, because how else can you explain it?

If you step back from your life for a minute and ask why you are working at your job, is it really because of some external motivator? Besides having to pay the bills and support yourself or a family, both external motivators, why are you at your present job? Is it because of the money? Possibly. Is it because of the commute? Possibly. The perks? Because you like the people? External motivation does have a bearing on your decision to be at your job—after all, you chose to be there. Your job did not find you; it appealed to you in some way. But once you are in your job, what motivates you to do well? Is it to show your boss how good you really are? This sounds like an internal motivation to me. Is it because you want to be the best? Sounds internal as well. Is it because you are just like that and have to perform at the very top levels? What about being a good team player, or wanting to be the go-to person everyone wants when he needs an answer, or when the chips are down? What about doing a good job just because that is who you are? All these are internal motivations.

Is someone going to perform well because of a paycheque? Well, the expectation is that you will perform acceptably to begin with, so I would say money is off the table. What about challenge? Is it the challenge itself, or is the challenge about stretching yourself and seeing whether you can do it? Close, but you have to want to take on the challenge, so I would say wanting to be challenged (internal) is the motivator instead of the challenge itself. It seems that all the external factors people name as the source of their motivation aren't the real motivation. In the end, you perform well not because of some carrot, but because it is in you to perform well at your job.[23]

The Manager's Role in Motivation

Is it the manager's job to motivate the staff to achieve her expectations? What if I told you that external motivation is overrated and employees need to motivate themselves? What if I told you that it is everyone's responsibility to motivate themselves? What if I said to you people who need to be motivated at their job need to find another job? Motivation only works for people who are internally motivated to do their job.[24] No amount of managing can motivate someone who doesn't care. Ever hear the saying, "You can lead a horse to water, but you can't make it drink?" That is what we are talking about here.

I once had a manager who told me what motivated him: money, challenge, and opportunity. I think those things will motivate most people, but they are all externally focused. Money will motivate for a time, but eventually the novelty will wear off, and you will be back where you were before. Challenge sounds interesting, but once the challenge becomes too chal-

---

23   "Finally there is the knowledge worker, and especially the advanced knowledge worker. . . . This means that no one can motivate him. He has to motivate himself. No one can direct him. He has to direct himself. Above all, no one can supervise him. He is the guardian of his own standards, of his own performance, and of his own objectives. He can be productive only if he is responsible for his own job." Drucker, Peter F. *The Frontiers of Management: Where Tomorrow's Decisions Are Being Shaped Today.* New York: Truman Talley, 1986. p. 196.

24   "The right people don't need to be tightly managed or fired up; they will be self-motivated by the inner drive to produce the best results and to be part of creating something great." Collins, James C. *Good to Great: Why Some Companies Make the Leap—and Others Don't.* New York, NY: Harper-Business, 2001. p. 42.

lenging will it still be a good motivator? Opportunity sounds a little self-serving, but if it gets you out of bed and into work in the morning, why not? But what if there is no opportunity?

The real question is, why does anyone need an external force to push him to do something? Why can't a worker meet the expectation because that is who he is and what he does? Why does a worker need to continually be offered inducements in order to perform? If there are objectives to be hit, workers should hit them! If a worker cannot immediately summon the motivation, a little bit of introspection should do the trick, and before he knows it, he should be doing great. However, it seems that this introspective ability is missing from poor performers.

The task of introspection seems to go to the manager. Instead of employees looking at themselves and understanding what they need to improve, the manager has to point out the problem and then come up with a plan to help the employees achieve whatever it is they lack.[25] This may work, but if the employee cannot figure out for herself what the issue is or even that there is a problem, how likely is it that this person will understand and execute your plan of action for her?

Today, managers are expected to motivate their employees, when in reality the employees need to motivate themselves. If someone cannot find internal motivation, then every external reason to do something will eventually fail. If that is true, what should a manager do? I say you cannot do anything. If your staff are not motivating themselves, no amount of external motivation will help. Poorly performing staff do not appear to self-motivate. They do not understand that they need to motivate themselves internally before a manager can motivate them with

---

25   Of the four core activities managers do, one is to "motivate the person by helping him identify and overcome his weakness." This is the traditional way great managers focus on strengths. The assumption of course is that the staff is capable and competent. Buckingham, Marcus, and Curt Coffman. *First, Break All the Rules: What the World's Greatest Managers Do Differently*. New York, NY: Simon & Schuster, 1999. pp. 66–67.

some type of inducement. This is similar to the idea that you need to love yourself before anyone will love you. If someone on your staff is missing this basic ingredient, no amount of anything will get them on the path of excelling at his job.

Performance Improvement Plans

Are Performance Improvement Plans Really About Improvement?

Whatever the term you use for performance improvement plans, one thing is consistent: they all deal with the same thing—poor performance. The stated goal of these plans is to help employees succeed[26] by giving them clear-cut goals and objective criteria to evaluate them against. For many people, the real use of a performance improvement plan is as the final nail in the coffin for getting rid of someone.

In a performance plan, you will set performance goals, determine what success looks like, and provide target dates for completion. If we consider this for a moment, we see that this seems to be a way to formalize the existing process of setting objectives. In Neil McPhie's report *Addressing Poor Performers and the Law* that was submitted to the Merit Systems Protection Board in September 2009 he describes a process where "The agency is required to articulate a performance expectation, measure it, and document the extent to which the employee has met or failed to meet expectations."[27] Isn't this already covered

---

26   "Regardless of the employee's occupational category, or any additional uses for the PIP, the purpose of the PIP is to provide the employee with the tools for success (where practical) and an opportunity to demonstrate that success." McPhie, Neil A.G., and Mary M. Rose. *Addressing Poor Performers and the Law*. Mspb.gov. U.S. Merit Systems Protection Board, 29 Sept. 2009. Web. Accessed 14 Feb. 2011.

27   McPhie, Neil A. G., and Mary M. Rose. *Addressing Poor Performers and the Law*. Mspb.gov. U.S. Merit Systems Protection Board, 29 Sept. 2009. Web. Accessed 14 Feb. 2011.

in the routine process of having a manager set objectives and evaluate her staff on them each year?

What is the difference between the performance improvement plan (PIP) and setting objectives? Sure, the goal of the PIP is to try to improve the performance of your poor performer, but if you set SMART objectives and have regular meetings with your staff about performance, what are you doing in the PIP that you are not already doing? It looks as if we are covering a lot of familiar ground here.

If you have only two formal meetings every year with your staff to discuss performance, that means a poor performer could be working for a year and a half before the manager finds it necessary (or possible) to do something about the poor performance. If you give the poor performer three chances to improve, at least a year passes before a performance improvement plan goes into action. A typical performance improvement plan usually lasts about three months, so you are looking at a year and three months before you can actually terminate if you opt to. What happens when the three months is over and the poor performer has improved? How long do you have to wait[28] before you go through this again? In your heart of hearts you know it is almost certainly a short-lived improvement.

If the poor performer improves, is he off the hook? Yes, he is off the hook until he puts himself on a performance plan again—and again. Does this process really add any value to the business or to your department? Continual performance improvement plans are a drain on resources, and all they achieve is to get someone to perform to the level he should have been performing at when he started the job. This seems somewhat

---

28   I have personally seen PIP's reoccur every six months for certain people. Hopefully, this is an anomaly. The U.S. Government under Chapter 43 of Title 5 of the U.S. Code states one year if performance improves and is maintained before another can be instituted. McPhie, Neil A. G., and Mary M. Rose. *Addressing Poor Performers and the Law*. Mspb. gov. U.S. Merit Systems Protection Board, 29 Sept. 2009. Web. Accessed 14 Feb. 2011.

counterintuitive to me. I could see the usefulness of a performance improvement plan if it took someone to the next level in his career, but this is not what is happening.

How do performance improvement plans address the underlying cause of poor performance? They don't. The performance improvement plan usually does not make concrete suggestions for skill improvement, such as increasing a worker's technical proficiency with a course, or improving her communication skills with a workshop.[29] Instead it usually takes the approach of having the worker hit certain targets, usually without any type of help or support from anyone else.

Maybe my cynical attitude is clouding my judgment, but I don't see why a PIP is necessary. If improvement is the goal, why formalize it? Why not just send Sandra on a course to upgrade her skills? If a PIP is such an important tool for performance management, why is there no well-defined standard for a PIP? As it stands now, any company can come up with its own version of a PIP. In fact, the only constants are timelines, expectations, and objectives. Training and support, however necessary, are not always included because often the company will not or cannot provide it.[30] Is that not interesting? This means that the PIP can in effect be perverted and the outcome steered to a foregone conclusion by the company failing to provide the services necessary to fulfill the tasks. If the point were truly to seek improvement, everything necessary to help the worker succeed would be provided as a matter of course, but this is often not the case. Why is that? I would surmise that deep down

29   "Remember, people don't change that much." Buckingham, Marcus, and Curt Coffman. *First, Break All the Rules: What the World's Greatest Managers Do Differently*. New York, NY: Simon & Schuster, 1999. pp. 80–82.

30   "When the agency is deciding what to place in the PIP, it is crucial that the agency only include that which the agency is prepared to actually provide." McPhie, Neil A. G., and Mary M. Rose. *Addressing Poor Performers and the Law*. Mspb.gov. U.S. Merit Systems Protection Board, 29 Sept. 2009. Web. Accessed 14 Feb. 2011.

people already know that the PIP is just there to confirm their opinion and get a poor performer one step closer to the exit.

The PIP is not really about improvement. We should call it a performance assessment (PA) because that is what is happening: you are assessing someone's performance to determine if they really need to be terminated or whether they can be allowed to stay with some remedial help. If we're assessing people, shouldn't everyone get one so the company can identify areas for improvement for all staff? I think this would be substantially more fair and useful. When the recommended approach is to "encourage supervisors to involve employees in the creation of the PIP whenever it is practical,"[31] that tells me improvement is not the real purpose of a PIP. A suggestion that "The employee may have a better sense of the source of the problem, or a better way to express the performance requirements, and therefore be able to help the supervisor to draft a PIP with a greater potential to result in improved performance"[32] just sounds like performance theatre. If the employee had a better sense of the problem, don't you think he should have come up with a solution before a PIP was even necessary? Also, it's odd that the employee is being asked to help define the performance requirement of the PIP when that same employee has already helped define his SMART objectives—and failed to meet them. Finally, who in his right mind is going to provide a performance requirement that he cannot reach, especially when his future depends on the successful completion of that PIP? The employee's goal is to not to improve his performance; it's to succeed in the PIP. What the manager is doing in this instance is making accommodations to produce the illusion of taking

31   McPhie, Neil A. G., and Mary M. Rose. *Addressing Poor Performers and the Law*. Mspb.gov. U.S. Merit Systems Protection Board, 29 Sept. 2009. Web. Accessed 14 Feb. 2011.

32   McPhie, Neil A. G., and Mary M. Rose. *Addressing Poor Performers and the Law*. Mspb.gov. U.S. Merit Systems Protection Board, 29 Sept. 2009. Web. Accessed 14 Feb. 2011.

action, and we all know that unintended consequences are now around the corner.

One of the other reasons I call a PIP "performance theatre" is that HR only becomes involved once someone has shown she cannot perform to an acceptable level. Until this point, the manager has been at the front lines dealing with this poor performance, and only now, when something serious needs to be done about it, does HR get involved. When it comes to giving yearly performance ratings, giving reprimands, or working with employees to create objectives, the manager is not second-guessed. Only when a termination is on the horizon does HR get involved. I am sure this is quite simply a case of the company covering itself against a lawsuit if they decide to terminate employment. If this really is the reason for the PIP, then let's forget the euphemisms and call a PIP what it really is. I think everyone would be much better off.

Let's say a widget maker is performing poorly, producing many defects and complications more than any other widget maker. The manager notices this and says, "We are putting you on a performance improvement plan because you are performing below par." Sounds like a good idea, right? He tells him, "We will provide you objectives to hit and timelines for improvement, and we'll check your performance at regular intervals. We'll even throw in a course or two on how to make widgets properly." Again, this sounds great, but what is the PIP doing about the poor performance? The widget maker still has to hit some type of performance target; maybe the only difference is the more formalized nature of the relationship. If the widget maker can reach the targets, he's worthy of keeping his job. If not, management has to make some decisions about his future in the organization. This sounds very similar to an assessment, which is "The evaluation or estimation of the nature, quality, or ability of someone, or something."[33]

If a PIP is really an assessment, we are weighing the playing field in favour of the company, because the only way the

---

33 *New Shorter Oxford English Dictionary.*

business can determine if someone is capable of doing her job is to have her achieve objectives related to her job. There is no test to show whether someone can do a job except doing the job within the acceptable parameters. If that is the criterion to determine acceptability, then all a PIP can do is rehash someone's objectives and then assesses that person on those very objectives. This is why I think all the PIP is doing is reinforcing the decision the manager made before the PIP was put into place: this person needs to go. The HR component is only there to formalize the decision. This really makes no sense, because if someone is performing poorly, and the company has already given her a few chances to improve, why force management to follow this process?

A Better Role for HR

I think it would be immensely more useful if HR, not just the manager, assessed the performance reviews of all staff and met with any workers identified as poor performers.[34] I believe it would be immensely useful if HR were actively involved at all stages of hiring. One of their jobs is to attract and retain talent, and it would be helpful they took a role in assessing dead weight and improving and if necessary terminating these people. Human resources deals with the employee, not necessarily the job function of the employee. To me it makes perfect sense for HR to meet with all staff and find out how they are coping in the job, whether there are any deficiencies, and what the company can do for them to improve certain aspects of their personality or work style to contribute better to the company. After all, HR brought these people into the organization; the least they could do is have an active role in their development.

---

34   HR should be actively involved in poor performance cases and not act in a passive role as was identified in *Addressing Poor Performers and the Law* and is probably the case in a majority of offices worldwide. McPhie, Neil A. G., and Mary M. Rose. *Addressing Poor Performers and the Law*. Mspb. gov. U.S. Merit Systems Protection Board, 29 Sept. 2009. Web. Accessed 14 Feb. 2011.

This relates to the concept of strategic human resource management. People are strategic resources in an organization: Without staff, nothing can be done, regardless of the organization. In the traditional resource-based view "an enterprise will usually train its employees to increase productivity."[35] I would think most people's understanding of the word "increase" in a business context means an improvement on the current production, i.e., making five widgets per hour instead of three. I do not believe there is any doubt about this interpretation. However, the same article describes training as ". . . pursuing other goals such as motivating employees, making employee promotion possible, upgrading their capabilities in order to access other job positions, and so on."[36] With poor performers, training is usually used to bring productivity up to baseline, not to bring productivity beyond it. So in this light it appears that the training has not reached its stated goal.

What chance does a poor performer have at truly upgrading her skill level when she cannot perform her job function at an appropriate level? I think the poor performer is lumped together with the competent group without any regard for her particular circumstance because of the underlying assumption that everyone is capable. In the resource-based theory, the term "competitive advantage" is also bandied about quite a lot. Essentially, this theory holds that staff is important, and it is one of the reasons why a company has the ability to outperform others in the same field. Functional capability[37] is regarded as a competitive advantage because it means knowledge and skill

35   Olalla, M. F. "The Resource-Based Theory and Human Resources." *International Advances in Economic Research*, 5(1):84–92. p. 89.

36   Olalla, M. F. "The Resource-Based Theory and Human Resources." *International Advances in Economic Research*, 5(1):84–92. p. 89.

37   "The ability to do specific things . . . proceeds from the knowledge, skills, and experience of employees and others in the value chain . . ." Olalla, M. F. "The Resource-Based Theory and Human Resources." *International Advances in Economic Research*, 5(1):84–92. p. 86.

is provided by a person.[38] Overall, these differences in knowledge, job execution, experience, and so on in their staff are the differentiating factors for organizations that help make them successful. What does this way of thinking imply for the poor performer?

If staff create a competitive advantage with their functional capability and are considered strategic because they are scarce, valuable, non-replicable, difficult to transfer, specific, etc.,[39] what is competitive about a someone who cannot achieve his objectives? Is a poor performer an essential employee or a scarce and valuable commodity?[40] What is strategic about developing a poor performer?

In a perfect world, HR and the manager should meet regularly to discuss staff performance and to design a training regimen for each worker so she can grow, improve, and add value to the organization. If this was a common task for HR, maybe they would come to realize that people who are interested in growing and improving, unlike the poor performer, typically work hard to assure they are performing at an acceptable level and are internally motivated to do their job well. At the very least, HR should have a host of tools at their disposal to assess employees. Once they identify the poor performers, perhaps HR can assess the problem and act accordingly, if of course they find value in doing that.

A PIP seems like a lot of wasted time and effort just to see whether someone is capable of doing their job. Maybe that is why no one does the other things discussed: it takes too much time and effort. A focused program of assessment and development would be a great program for people identified as up and coming, or those on a promotion trajectory. Although I think

38   Olalla, M. F. "The Resource-Based Theory and Human Resources." *International Advances in Economic Research*, 5(1):84–92. p. 86.

39   Olalla, M. F. "The Resource-Based Theory and Human Resources." *International Advances in Economic Research*, 5(1):84–92. p. 87.

40   Olalla, M. F. "The Resource-Based Theory and Human Resources." *International Advances in Economic Research*, 5(1):84–92. p. 87.

poor performers would get some very real benefit out of such a program, it is almost certain that they will never be given the opportunity to be involved because it would be expensive in both time and effort. If this training and development were to be the company norm, it would go to those who are considered good or great employees because why would anyone spend that much time and effort on someone who potentially has no future in the organization? So the question companies need to ask is, will we fix people's problems so they can do their jobs, or will we hire people to who can already do the job and then let them do it?

Do PIPs Really Help Anybody Become a Good Employee?

If we are truly interested in having people improve so they can become good employees, is a PIP the right way to go about this? Can a PIP bring someone's performance to an acceptable level that is then sustained? How high does the success rate have to be in order for the PIP to be considered a worthwhile exercise? When some of the success stories end up doing another performance plan in a few months[41] because they fell back into their old work habits, it suggests that the PIP is more of a fear-based weapon than a useful tool.

This goes back to the individual. The poor performer seems to have a "flaw," but the PIP does nothing to fix this underlying problem because it can't. Successfully completing the PIP shows that competence is possible and that the poor perfor-

---

41 "In some instances, a PIP can be requested every year or at a shorter time interval, depending on the rules and the organization. Usually, a PIP has a sustained performance window and if performance drops outside of that window a subsequent PIP is necessary, following the same rules as before." The most I have ever seen was two in less than a year before termination. The U.S. Government under Chapter 43 of Title 5 of the U.S. Code states 1 year if performance improves and is maintained before another can be instituted. McPhie, Neil A. G., and Mary M. Rose. *Addressing Poor Performers and the Law.* Mspb.gov. U.S. Merit Systems Protection Board, 29 Sept. 2009. Web. Accessed 14 Feb. 2011.

mance is a decision, albeit an unconscious one, not to perform to the stated expectation. If a worker can perform, but only with maximum supervision on each task, I do not think you can consider him the right person.[42]

Assessing the Value of PIPs within Your Company

Am I willing to say that a PIP does not add any value in the grand scheme of things? Maybe the PIP could add value if it were redesigned, but in its current form I really cannot see how a PIP adds value, especially if it will determine a potential termination of employment. As we asked earlier, how successful does a PIP need to be in order for it to be considered a successful tool? That is a question each company needs to answer on its own, but I cannot see how we can consider a process with a potentially high failure rate as something useful to the company, nor something with a potentially high success rate in the context of a poor performer, especially if there is a revolving door of participants.

What does it mean when most people on a PIP fail it? If, on the other hand, most of the people on a PIP improve what would that mean? What does it say about the entire process if those very people who improved are back in three, six, nine, or twelve months on another PIP? Are we prepared to accept that maybe there is something wrong with the way we manage or the way we articulate our expectations? No one likes to have the blame placed at her doorstep, especially when it comes to performance, but managers do play a role in the performance of their staff, and they need to be sure all the "right things" are being done. I think if a person has SMART objectives and

---

42 "The moment you feel the need to tightly manage someone, you've made a hiring mistake. The best people don't need to be managed. Guided, taught, led—yes. But not tightly managed." Collins, James C. *Good to Great: Why Some Companies Make the Leap—and Others Don't.* New York, NY: HarperBusiness, 2001. p. 56.

understands exactly what his manager expects of him day in and day out, then the responsibility for his performance rests squarely on his shoulders and it ends there.

Providing Useful and Meaningful Feedback

What Purpose Does Feedback Serve?

Feedback is a way to help someone improve her performance in a given situation or task. Regardless of how the feedback is conveyed, the main point is that it has to be relevant and timely in order to be effective in helping someone improve her performance.[43] A person interested in advancing in his career sees feedback as essential, as long as it is constructive. The poor performer usually has a different understanding regarding feedback and its purpose. The poor performer may believe her manager is the problem, and that feedback received from him is irrelevant. She may interpret the feedback as personal criticism instead of seeing it as a vehicle for improvement. Most probably, she will interpret negative feedback as "getting in trouble" and respond with resentment.

If poor performers are unwilling to receive feedback in a positive way,[44] what purpose does it serve to offer them feedback? We have all heard the expression "don't waste your breath," but that is exactly what you as the manager are doing in this case. Feedback only works as long as the person who receives it is interested in changing or improving, and poor performers usually are

---

43   "It must be timely. It must be relevant. It must be operational. It must focus on his job." Drucker, Peter F. *The Frontiers of Management: Where Tomorrow's Decisions Are Being Shaped Today.* New York: Truman Talley, 1986. p. 190.

44   "Feedback that is provided for development should encourage the feedback recipient to desire accurate feedback, which should make the individual more receptive to negative feedback." Silverman, S. B., C. E. Pogson, and A. B. Cober. "When Employees at Work Don't Get It: A Model for Enhancing Individual Employee Change in Response to Performance Feedback." *Academy of Management Executive,* 19(2):135–147.

not interested in either. They already believe they are competent at what they do, or they do not see the purpose behind feedback, so they reject it outright, or they are so incompetent they cannot take the direction offered and turn it into any meaningful result.

Feedback is one of a manager's most powerful tools, but like most things it is only powerful if it means something to the receiving party.[45] So now you are in a quandary. On the one hand you have to provide feedback because that is what managers do; however, your feedback is worthless because the poor performer does not see any value in that feedback. One of the things we managers need to understand is how to talk to our staff. You have to find a way to communicate with your poor performer, and the only way is verbally, because an email just does not do feedback justice.

Direct feedback is best, but if the listener does not understand what you are trying to say, how direct is that communication? Remember, it is not what you say, it is how you are saying it—but more important, how the other party interprets it—that counts. How often have you said one thing and found that your staff members understood something else? Feedback is doubly difficult because you have to talk about performance, corrective measures, or helpful insight, none of which a poor performer is very interested in to begin with. As well, you are in the uncomfortable situation of having to say to someone that he is not performing adequately. So you might reasonably find that the feedback you offer is not entirely clear to the receiving party.

Suppose someone is not performing to standard. There are several ways to say that, all of which are somewhat open to interpretation. For instance: "I need you to step up your game"; "your current work is unsatisfactory and I need you to be better"; "you have not improved enough"; "your work can use some improvement"; or "this is not what I asked for." Most people would read those comments and realize that they

---

45   Read Section II: "Your Words and How They Trigger Action and Reaction" for a better understanding of this. Malandro, Loretta A. *Say It Right the First Time.* New York: Mcgraw-Hill, 2003. pp. 79–167.

need to improve, but interpretation is a very strange thing. People interpret things based on their own life experience and what they understand words to mean, and remember that not everyone understands the same words in the same way.[46] With the examples above, let's take a look at how else we can interpret those comments:

- "I need you to step up your game." This means improve, but does it say, "you are not performing to the standard"? The person may understand it to mean she is doing well, but she needs to excel for a time, which is a valid interpretation because there is no context provided. What might have been better is, "You are not performing up to standard; I need you to step up your game," but even this suggests that only recently the person has not met the standard. What could have been better still is, "You have not been providing me with satisfactory results since you started. I need you to step up your game starting now."

- "Your current work is satisfactory; I just need you to be quicker." This is an ambiguous statement; on the one hand things are fine, yet they are not fine. This is a mixed signal. More than likely the poor performer will continue to do whatever he is doing, since the quality of the work is fine, it's just the speed at which he does it that is an issue. In the mind of a poor performer, you can have one or the other, but you cannot have both.

- "You have not improved enough." This means she has improved. Again, it is a very weak statement. Poor performers need to know in an unequivocal way they are

---

46 "Communication is much more involved, and once you add the dimension of power and authority, the problem compounds. Leaders must work through an intricate maze of how others filter, interpret, and add personal meaning to their messages. Malandro, Loretta A. *Say It Right the First Time.* New York: Mcgraw-Hill, 2003. p. 5.

below standard. Saying they have not improved enough means they have improved somewhat, which has to be taken into consideration. Because the statement is rather ambiguous, it is difficult to understand whether improvement is too little or just below expectation. The poor performer will understand that she has improved even if she has not. More than likely the poor performer heard the word "improved" and nothing else, so your entire message is worthless.

- "Your work can use some improvement." Again, this means things are not that bad. Things probably are bad, but the poor performer interprets this as meaning that things are okay and he only has to improve a little. This means things are not that serious, and the poor performer will not make the changes or will make only a poor attempt at change.

- None of these results reflect the intention of the feedback, but as you can see, interpretation can vary widely.[47]

I suspect most managers give poor performers ambiguous feedback because they are uncomfortable with the situation. The only way to make your point is to overcome your discomfort and articulate in no uncertain terms that things are unacceptable. Examples of this kind of statement are: "Your performance is unacceptable; you have not accomplished the necessary tasks." "You did not complete the task in the time allotted." Note the negative[48] tone to these examples. The previous examples were

---

47   Malandro, Loretta A. *Say It Right the First Time*. New York: Mcgraw-Hill, 2003. pp. 80–109.

48   Although I do not generally agree with using euphemisms with poor performers, Malandro does point out that it is possible to provide negative feedback in a positive way. However, my assumption is this suggestion is directed toward staff who are competent, since she says, "Unless you are ready to fire the individual, paint a positive picture of what you want."

geared to being positive, which is fine if encouragement to do better is the goal. But with a poor performer, the goal is to get them to an acceptable level of performance.

If the goal of your feedback is to steer the poor performer toward an acceptable level of performance, is it best served by encouragement? Feedback can do two things: either bring the person up, or bring them down. Positive feedback focuses on the good with an emphasis on improving to reach a certain level. Negative feedback is all about what you did not accomplish; it points out what was deficient. Of the two, I am sure almost everyone would prefer to focus on the positive and gently instruct people and point them in the right direction to discover for themselves how they need to improve, but I suspect you probably have already tried that and found that it has not worked.

Telling someone she is not doing her job may sound negative, but it is the truth. There is no point in trying to sugar-coat the truth about someone's work performance.[49] That does not mean being insensitive, but it can seem that way. If a poor performer is not doing her job and cannot be introspective enough to understand she is not capable, being pleasant and being ambiguous is not helping her. If you want someone to understand what you are saying, be blunt. This may be the wakeup call that she actually needs. Direct, unambiguous feedback is best.

Honest Feedback

What is honest feedback, and what purpose does it serve? Honest feedback is not an opportunity to berate every negative aspect of someone's personality or work ethic. That really has no purpose in a work environment and can only be done on

---

Malandro, Loretta A. *Say It Right the First Time*. New York: Mcgraw-Hill, 2003. p. 99.

49 "Sugarcoating the truth about subpar performance is disrespectful and unfair; people need regular and candid feedback on how well they are doing." Axlerod, Beth, Helen Handfield-Jones, and Ed Michaels. "A New Game Plan for C Players." *Harvard Business Review*, Jan 2002. p. 87.

your way out the door, never to return. Is honest feedback valid? It may be the ramblings of a disgruntled employee or very insightful observations. For instance, imagine a poor performer who continually inputs data incorrectly. This person's error rate is 30% higher than the average, and he is the worst person on the five-person team. You might be tempted to say to that person, "You might as well have hooves for hands for all the errors you're making!" Although this statement would be honest in some sense, I would not call it feedback.

The test of good feedback is this: does it offer help in fixing the issue or identify some aspect of the person's work that causes her to have so many errors? The statement in the last paragraph may illustrate that the person is bad, but it doesn't provide any instruction on how to improve. Is the purpose to put fear in your staff, show your superiors you are a no-nonsense boss, or are you just an asshole who enjoys belittling people? There has to be a reason for doing what you are doing. If the feedback is not designed to help staff improve or identify a gap needing to be closed through training or something else, then why bring it up in the first place?

Does the statement "You are the worst in the group" count as honest feedback? It does, but what is the point of the statement if there is nothing constructive to discuss about it? It is far more useful to say, "Your error rate is consistently 30% more than the rest of the group, and I notice that 80% of those errors are in two fields. I think it might be a good idea to talk to the group and find out how they overcame that issue, or if they had those issues in the past." This is much better. It is specific, relevant to the issue, and gives the person an opportunity to figure out the problem and modify his execution of the job on his own. The metrics that revealed the errors to begin with would track an improvement in the next round of metrics. If you see this improvement, you can say, "I see that your error rate has dropped by 10%, and you have reduced your error rate on those two fields by 50%. You are doing well since we last talked. How else do you feel you can improve your performance?" If things did not improve: "I see you have not improved since we last met. You error rates are still the same, and your difficultly with those two fields is still your greatest problem. Did you speak with the group about it?" Now, we hope, a discussion about performance follows and if the person is genuinely interested in improving, he will. If he is not, the conversation can take on a different tone.

This feedback is honest, direct, and unambiguous, all within the confines of being civil. If you were one of those bosses who relished instilling fear, you could have easily said something similar to, "What the hell are you doing? Your error rate is 30 fucking percent higher than everyone else's. What the fuck is that all about? Either you get your shit together and start doing your fucking job properly, or I will personally walk you out of the goddamn building because you won't be working here anymore!"[50] That conveys the message that improvement is needed in no uncertain terms, but does it really make the employee want to go out and give her best?

Continual Negative Performance Feedback

Hopefully, no manager will lose her temper with an employee to the point of saying something like that, yet I am sure there are many managers who would love to let loose with a barrage of comments like those out of sheer frustration. If the manager provides continual appropriate feedback, this type of outburst is unlikely. But, after the second poor performance rating in a row, shouldn't the poor performer say to himself, "I need to do better"? Yet we know poor performers

---

50 "All too often, persons in authority tend to criticize subordinates only when they are upset, angry, and no longer able to hold their tempers in check. As a result, the negative feedback they provide is neither specific (i.e., focused on particular past behaviors) nor considerate. On the contrary, because of the criticizer's strong emotions, it is typically delivered in a biting, sarcastic tone, and includes threats and other negative features." Baron, Robert A. "Negative Effects of Destructive Criticism: Impact on Conflict, Self-Efficacy, and Task Performance." *Journal of Applied Psychology*, 73(2). p.199.

continue to receive unacceptable performance ratings regardless of the feedback provided.

If someone does not have the awareness to understand that she is not performing to an acceptable level, or have the ability to bring her performance to an acceptable level even after she is given direct, unambiguous feedback, why should this person still be considered an asset to the company? Given this situation, does it make sense to keep providing feedback? Unfortunately, you do not have a choice. As a manager, one of the things you have to do is provide feedback, even when you know it is not doing any good. Eventually, it gets us a date with HR to discuss a performance improvement plan.

Getting Rid of the Poor Performer

Let Them Be Someone Else's Problem?

To me, it makes no sense to deal with the situation by moving a poor performer to another position or another department. I fully understand why people do this. Although they also know it is not a good idea, they just cannot cope with the poor performer. Why does anyone consider pawning a poor performer off on someone else to be an acceptable option? When nothing is working with the poor performer, and there is nothing left you can do, a typical human response is to get rid of the problem. We find the fastest and easiest way to get it dealt with, and that is to let it be someone else's problem.

I have to admit, I am guilty of this. I did it knowing full well what I was doing, and that it would not help the person in question. After I realized I would not be able to terminate this person, I tried to make him someone else's problem. It did not work. Everyone knew about this person's personality and work habits, so nobody would take him when I suggested he might be better suited to a different management style, or to a work environment where his natural analytical abilities could shine. This person did not get accepted for any of the internal jobs he applied for either. He was a poor performer, and moving him to a new environment would have just moved the problem somewhere else.

If They Cannot Do It, Let Someone Else Do It?

How often have you had to reassign a task to someone else to get it finished—or started for that matter? We have all seen this happen, especially in situations that are critical to safety or extremely time sensitive. If you have ever done this, this tells me you are someone who expects her staff to perform and hit their targets. Nobody likes a weak link on her team and if you find yourself continually reassigning tasks or giving the really hard or critical projects to the same people, you have a weak link. The question then is, how weak is the weak link?

Not everybody can be the best. I think we all understand that. But when there is a significant discrepancy in skill between members of a team, then there is a problem. If everyone had the same skill set, work ethic, and ability to execute his job, then everything would be equal. Everyone would be the same from a working perspective, and we could assign tasks evenly and complete them within the same time frame no matter who was assigned.

As we all know, this is practically never the case. What happens instead is that there is a variance between the members of the team. If the variance between the team members is minor, then you are lucky: everyone in the team can participate fully, and all members of the team can pull their weight. When this is not the case, the higher achieving members of the team can end up carrying the low performers to get things done. If someone is consistently poor in relation to the other team members, the manager must decide what the right decision is. Maybe it is termination, maybe not. At the end of the day, the decision about what to do is up to the manager. At least now he can make the decision with his eyes wide open. There are consequences for every decision, but some consequences are easier to live with than others.[51]

---

51 ". . . poor performers can also take managers into difficult ethical

Firing the Poor Performer

Is it too much to expect a consistently acceptable level of performance from an employee? I do not think so and I do not think many other people expect less either. When a person accepts employment from a company, the company at the very least expects that person to perform to her manager's expectations, or to an acceptable standard. We have shown poor performers cannot make the grade because of some internal issue to them,[52] and that no amount of managing will do anything to change that. If that is the case, how can anyone conclude that such a person should continue employment with any company?

As you can see there are many variables to deal with regarding a poor performer, but if your gut and your objective measures are telling you to do something, and you can live with your conscience, you cannot ignore the option of termination forever. I am not conflicted about termination. If it is necessary, then it needs to be done quickly. Lingering on such a decision creates other problems down the road.[53]

Unfortunately the process of terminating with cause is

---

decisions that they may not be equipped to deal with, such as choices between termination and staff development and, more fundamentally, between justice and mercy." Goodhew, Geoffrey W., Peter A. Cammock, and Robert T. Hamilton. "The Management of Poor Performance by Front-Line Managers." Journal of Management Development, 27(9). p. 952. Originally in Cranston, N., L. C. Chrich, and M. Kimber, (2006), "Ethical dilemmas: the 'bread and butter' of educational leaders' lives." *Journal of Educational Administration*, 44(2):106–21.

52   "They found that poor performers vastly overestimate themselves and show deficient metacognitive skills in comparison with their more skilled counterparts." Kruger, Justin, and David Dunning. "Unskilled and Unaware—but Why? A Reply to Krueger and Mueller (2002)." *Journal of Personality & Social Psychology*, 82(2). p. 189.

53   "Letting the wrong people hang around is unfair to all the right people, as they inevitably find themselves compensating for the inadequacies of the wrong people. Worse, it can drive away the best people. Strong performers are intrinsically motivated by performance, and when they see their efforts impeded by carrying extra weight, they eventually become

usually long and drawn-out, not to mention that the requirement of documenting a person's performance is a very difficult task.[54] The difficulty of terminating with cause can make this course of action infeasible. Luckily, termination with cause is not the only avenue open when termination is the right decision.

Cost of Terminating without Cause

Termination without cause is a very viable option and has undoubtedly been used ever since there was a person in a subordinate position failing to meet someone's expectations. This is the reality we live in. There are numerous reasons why a manager would terminate someone without cause. Such a termination should not necessarily be viewed in a negative light. We just need to recognize it for what it is: a tool.

Sometimes terminating without cause is the most efficient and humane way to deal with a poor performer, but of course any tool can be used for good or bad. When evaluating it as an option for termination, we should keep that in mind, because even though a manager may think he is being objective about terminating someone, without some sort of "due process," the decision can be very subjective. When the decision to terminate without cause is made, the reasons need to be identified up front so the appropriate compensation can be meted out to the terminated employee to ensure everyone is satisfied.[55]

---

frustrated." Collins, James C. *Good to Great: Why Some Companies Make the Leap—and Others Don't.* New York, NY: HarperBusiness, 2001. p. 56.

54 "Respondents told us that the most difficult task for supervisors was to document the employee's performance (39 percent reporting difficulty), followed by defending the decision to demote or remove the employee (37 percent), and discussing the performance deficiencies with the employee (36 percent). Fewer than a third of supervisors cited the difficulty of developing a PIP or supervising employees under a PIP (31 percent each). Our 2009 survey found somewhat similar results." U.S. Merit Systems Protection Board. "Removing Poor Performers in the Federal Service," p.8. Available at www.mspb.gov.

55 I worked in an office where my manager at the time was attempting to make a case for the termination of a 25-year employee. This person

If we decide to use termination without cause—euphemistically called "paying someone to leave"—how expensive will it be?[56] If we assume it takes 24 hours for the manager to decide to terminate someone without cause, what steps are needed to complete the process and how long will they take?

HR creating the paperwork: let's say 2 days. (I have seen situations where HR completed the paperwork and created the cheque in under 3 hours.)

1. HR and the manager doing the termination: roughly 30 minutes.

2. Terminating access: one hour.

3. Telling the team of said person's departure: 10 minutes.

4. Sending a note about the person's departure to the company at large (if your company does that): 10 minutes.

5. Creating or reapplying a job description to hire new staff: 1 hour.

6. HR posting the position: 1 day.

7. Waiting for resumes: 1–3 weeks.

8. Searching through resumes: 2 days.

9. Shortlisting and interviewing: 1–3 weeks.

---

never had a documented issue of performance for his entire career even though in his current job he was very inadequate. The option to terminate without cause was decided to be the fastest and best course of action. The end result was that the person was let go, but his compensation package was more than adequate to prevent a lawsuit or any ill will. In the end the person won, and the manager got what he wanted.

56   We are moving to the realm of legal issues. Do yourself a favour and consult HR and the company lawyer if you plan to take this course of action. This is definitely a case of *covering your ass*. The question boils down to how much money has to be paid to ensure this person will leave and not sue.

10. Waiting for the new hire to arrive: 2 weeks.

We are looking at anywhere from two to eight weeks for a new hire to come through the door. I think that is pretty reasonable, depending on the job. It takes time for someone to get up to speed—let's say around three months—and during that time, the remaining team members have to pick up the slack. However, they have been doing that for a while, so there should be no problem there. Assuming that you hired well and the new person is better than the one you let go, I would think you should start to see a difference within six to eight weeks of the new hire coming on board.

So how much money is it going to cost to terminate without cause? The following is my estimated breakdown. For simplicity, let's use a standard salary of $100,000 per year for everyone involved, which works out to $1,923 per week, $384 per day, and $48 per hour.

1. Manager's time: $6,000–$17,000 (3–8 weeks).

2. HR manager's time: $2,000 (1 week).

3. Recruiting fee: $20,000 (estimate).

4. Getting up to speed: $12,000 (6 weeks).

5. Staff getting new hires up to speed: $15,000 (8 weeks).

6. Setting up a computer, desk, phone, parking pass, access card, etc.: $500.00.

The total is $55,500–$66,500 to bring someone on and have her be productive.

7. Termination payout: let's say 1 month's salary ($7,692) for every year employed by the company, but this could be more or less depending on numerous variables.[57]

---

57 Remember, this is just an estimate. After talking with legal council, this figure could be more or less.

» Three years: $23,000 dollars.
» Five years: $38,460 dollars.

This gives us a grand total of about $100,000 dollars to terminate an employee without cause, hire someone else, and bring them up to speed. Yes, this is an overly generous estimate because we know a manager is not going to use every minute of the day dealing with hiring someone new nor is HR, but we can at least use it as a baseline.

Does it make sense to remove the poor performer sooner instead of later? From a financial perspective, I would say yes. If nothing else, terminating him sooner saves you money on his termination payout. From a productivity perspective, I would also say yes. It is cheaper in the long run to terminate a poor performer quickly and hire new talent that will perform better. As I have said before, people inherently know when someone is good or bad at his job. Once you make that determination and decide to terminate, do it. Don't let the decision fester with time. The faster you make the decision and "pay them to leave," the faster things will return to a new normal. No one will miss the person for long, if at all. Everyone is replaceable.

5

What Should You Do?

Changing How We Think about Poor Performance

Should We Hold the Manager Responsible?

Have you ever wondered whether you are responsible for another person's poor performance?

Most people familiar with hockey would say Wayne Gretzky is the greatest hockey player in the history of the game. Is he great because he had great coaching? Coaches played a role in helping him refine his skills and identify areas of improvement, but at the end of the day, it was his natural skill, ability, experience, and training that created a level of task execution that brought him 61 NHL records.[58] The other part to that is motivation—the internal motivation of striving to be the best. You can have all the talent in the world, but if you don't have the drive to be the best, you will not. Conversely, if you have the drive to be the best and work to become the best, you can

---

58 Nhl.com. "NHL Records Held or Shared by Wayne Gretzky" http://www.nhl.com/ice/news.htm?id=384583.

achieve your goals as long as you have the requisite ability, skills, and potential.

Sure, there was the support structure that allowed him to be his best, but that is another topic. From a performance perspective, you cannot say the coach did a bad job, so he had a bad game. I do not think I have ever heard that in my life. Players have good days and bad days, and you can tell when you watch them play their game. In the working world, it is no different. People do their jobs by themselves. They may report to someone or be on a team, but in the end they are the ones who do the work. Someone other than the person doing the work, i.e., a coach or manager, assesses whether it is acceptable. To suggest Wayne Gretzky is great because of the people who coached him lessens the emphasis on his personal accomplishment, will, and hard work and implies he is only great because of external forces—that he is not fully responsible for his accomplishments. Yes, people recognized his skills and his abilities and helped him along the way by allowing him to get to professional level hockey, but his skill and determination were all his. The same goes for staff.

Good performers are good because they work hard and have it in them to be good. Taking credit for the performance of a good performer at work is much the same as a coach claiming responsibility for the greatness of Wayne Gretzky. And if we managers cannot claim individual responsibility for the success of our staff, why are we saddled with the responsibility for the poor performance of individual staff? As managers, we are responsible for getting results, and I fully agree with that, but you cannot expect someone to be truly responsible for someone else's performance. You can dangle carrots in front of poor performers to try to motivate them; you can mentor them and train them, but if they can't do the job, they can't do the job. And if they won't do the job, they won't do the job.

This goes back to one of my earlier points. If your job is to get results, then your team must be up to the challenge. Yes, the manager is responsible for the overall achievement of those goals, but how well people work is up to them. Good performers get things done; poor performers find excuses. The manager's responsibility is about the result. The employee's responsibility is to do her job to an acceptable standard and within the time allotted. Responsibility for the results of that performance, either good or bad, rests squarely on the shoulders of the manager, which is why it is in the best interest of the manager to get rid of a poor performer and have a team who can get the job done.

Is Poor Performance the Result of Bad Management?

I am sure you have heard this statement at some point: A person's performance is poor because you are not managing them properly. Do you believe that? If your expectations are attainable and your management is working for everyone on the team except one person, doesn't that suggest that this person is the problem, not you?

Poor performers may already be working to the best of their abilities. We have discussed the role of natural ability earlier, but I think we need to mention it again. If they are maxing out their abilities and are still inadequate, additional management effort is futile. The manager should know the limits of her staff, and consider whether effort put into management will be well spent.

"If you manage them, they will improve," you are told. Improvement is meaningless if the worker will never reach an adequate level. Instead of wasting time and effort on this lost cause, just hire staff who can do the job. Some of you may think this is taking the easy way out instead of managing, but management is a difficult job, and wasting effort on the wrong solution will not help. If management is all you need, why are poor performers so poor? Did management make these workers that way in the first place? If so, why does poor performance only affect a small group—typically one to three employees—in any given department? If everyone else can work to standard and they cannot, I really don't think management is the direct cause that some people think it is.

I would say management accounts for about 10% of performance. If someone is underperforming by a larger margin, it is not because of how we are managing them, it is because of issues internal to that person.

Is Their Poor Performance a Reflection on You?

When you do nothing about a poor performer, it gets noticed. Everyone is looking at the manager and wondering what's going on. If you are seen to be acting as if everything is fine, then real scorn and anger will eventually be directed at you. Initially, people blame the poor performer, but over time the manager bears the brunt of the hostility. Pray that people like you enough that some of the anger is deflected, but there will be anger. Comments like this one will abound: "He is a nice person and I have nothing against him personally but he isn't doing a damn thing about that crappy employee!" When people start talking about your performance as a manager in a bad light, then you have a very real problem. Unless you do something drastic, your stock in the company will slowly drop. Upper management may consider you a nice person, but when they need a solid manager to take on a special project, they won't choose you. Your perceived lack of effectiveness in managing the performance of your staff will make upper management wonder if you are really up to the task.

As long as you are doing something, like mentoring or using a PIP to try to make the poor performer improve his performance, the worker will be seen as the problem and you will be viewed with sympathy. Poor old you, you have to deal with a poor performer; you have put your manager hat on and coached, lectured, and mentored. Your fellow managers can see that you are doing everything in your power, and nothing is working. Management no longer talks about you behind your back as a manager who cannot manage but as a manager who has a problem that none of them want.

If you can turn the situation around and transform this person into a competent employee, you will be the envy of all, and even attract a raised eyebrow or two from the levels above. People will be interested and curious about how you did it—not to mention impressed. From here promotion is sure to follow according to the current thought process. But how long are you willing to work on this problem before logic and reason tell you it is time to abandon hope? This will depend on many variables, but everyone can determine on some level how much time is too much time, especially when their performance can affect you and your reputation within an organization.

I was in a meeting once when my boss's boss told to me I should be proud of the steps I was taking to get one of my staff back on track instead of terminating them. I remarked off the cuff that she was improving, but not by much. His look said it all. I had definitely said something he did not want to hear. Not only was I expected to "fix" this problem, I also felt that he wanted me to accept this struggle and wear it as a badge of honour, as if I had been through the wars and would ultimately be better for it. I do not buy that. To me, it was wasted effort that had no real benefit to speak of.

In the end, management measures you on achieving your objectives. You only get credit for helping your employees improve insofar as it helps you reach your objectives, and although staff development is important, it is not a major component of anyone's objectives. The results you achieve are the basis of your bonus, potential promotion, and raise. Rehabilitating a poor performer may be something that gets praised, but if you were to survey every CEO and ask them to pick one: a rise in profit, or a rise in staff skill level, which one would they choose? The profit. This means it is essential to assemble a team who can consistently get you the results you need. The poor performer has no place on your team or in the company.

Is It Worth Trying to Improve the Poor Performer?

Will a Poor Performer Improve?

A poor performer cannot improve very much and does not come to the table with a high level of skill either. How do we label this? How about the "Fredo syndrome," after the character of Fredo in *The Godfather*. A little tongue-in-cheek, sure, but if you have seen the Godfather movies, you will know what I am talking about. Fredo is not self-aware, nor is he good at being a gangster, although he thinks he is. He cannot hold a candle to either his brother Michael or the other members of the family.

Many poor performers are very nice people, but this is not what we are talking about. This has to do with how these people[59] are built from the get-go. The question is, do they have the skills and the tools to be competent in their job, and the answer is, I really do not think so. Poor performers cannot achieve a given level of job performance, and I think they are not designed to. It may be possible for them to reach a lower standard, but they cannot meet the current standard set by their manager, nor are they likely to.[60]

If poor performance is truly some type of internal flaw, what can the manager or the company do about it? I do not know

---

59 Chronic poor performers are not a class of individual. They are people who cannot and have not met their manager's expectations. This includes a host of people from all walks of life and all types of jobs. Their common feature is that they cannot meet or exceed the given expectations of them at their place of employ. That is not to say they cannot excel somewhere else; they just cannot meet the expectations set out for them in their current job.

60 "Some managers erroneously believe that all C performers can be developed into B or even A performers and that the organization should invest in people indefinitely for this to happen." Axlerod, Beth, Helen Handfield-Jones, and Ed Michaels. "A New Game Plan for C Players." *Harvard Business Review*, Jan 2002. p. 82. Print.

whether anyone can do anything about it, because it depends on the person's internal motivation, skills, talent, and abilities. How can a manager motivate a worker to do better when he does not have it in him to reach the standard set out for him? It is beginning to look as if people vary in their ability to meet performance standards. Sure, we can set standards so low that everyone is capable of meeting them. Does anyone really think this should be the expected practice in any environment? What kind of message does that send to workers in the company, and how can management make any demands or distinctions when it has made a practice of lowering standards to accommodate everyone? In my more cynical moments, I think someone will eventually classify poor performance as an ailment, and it will be the company's responsibility to deal with it as such. Perhaps it will be listed in the *Diagnostic and Statistical Manual of Mental Disorders* (DSM IV) as Cognitive Labour Deficiency Syndrome.

In hockey, what happens when someone is not performing? He either plays on the poorer lines, or he is benched, put in the minors, or traded. I believe this is one of the reasons sports resonate with people so much: they are all about performance. In golf, the top ten people are usually the ones who were the top ten last week and will be top ten next week. In business, we do not bench people. We may demote them on occasion, but I have not seen that happen in all my years of working. Instead, we expect that a poor performer will eventually find her stride and start performing well.

Why do we think this? According to *First, Break All The Rules*, people can't change that much. If we already know this and accept it, why do we create and execute a process that appears to be an exercise in failure? It is to verify our assumptions or to give it that good old college try? Do we really believe that people can become substantially better, or are we just following the accepted norm when it comes to poor performance? It seems counterintuitive to me. We give a poor performer more than one chance to prove himself, and if he fails, we help him the next time. If he fails again, we send him on some training to make him better, and give him yet another chance. I agree with giving someone a second chance, but if you have eyes, you will see that giving him the second chance will have same result as the first. It's unfortunate that this management pattern, based on our stubborn belief that a poor performer can reach expectation, appears to be the norm.

What benefit is the company getting out of trying to help poor performers improve? If you go to the store, buy a product, take it home, use it, and then find out that it is defective, what do you do? Do you keep it, hoping that it will eventually start working properly? Or perhaps you try to fix it. How long will it be before you stop trying to make it work and return it for a working one? People don't hold on to things that don't work; yet with employees who cannot perform we do not seem to have the same thought processes.

Considering the Best Use of Company Resources

If we care about the staff who perform well and are interested in their ability to advance, what about poor performers? Do we care about them the same way we care about those who actually make the grade? Often poor performers receive the most attention, when it should actually be the other way around.[1] Those who need the most time, attention, and resources from a company are the ones who end up providing the least amount of value; does this make sense to anybody?

Does it make sense for a business run for profit to use company resources to try to get poorly performing staff members to an acceptable level when there have been no indications since they were hired that they can meet their manager's expectations? People usually spend extra money to get something better than what they have, not to get what they should already have; spending money to have someone become accept-

---

1   "Managers should spend the most time with their best people." Buckingham, Marcus, and Curt Coffman. *First, Break All the Rules: What the World's Greatest Managers Do Differently.* New York, NY: Simon & Schuster, 1999. pp. 153–154.

able seems like a waste when the return is substantially less than what other performers can provide. Improvement is good, but if the improvement only gets someone to where he should already be, is this an improvement in real terms? The worker has not provided added value or taken on greater responsibility, nor has there been a gain in trust or any significant increase in productivity. Using extra resources in an attempt to improve the performance level of poor performing staff is still a bad value proposition.

Resources are finite; how should you spend them? It makes the most sense to spend the money in ways that increase revenue or make the company more efficient. When you spend your finite resources on your staff, what do you think? Does spending money on a poor performer to bring them up to the performance level of the average staff member increase revenue or making a business more efficient?

Poor performers have at their disposal many resources to help them reach their potential. I am not saying that this is necessarily a bad thing: I am saying that if resources are scarce, why not spend them on things that will give you the most benefit? A simple example is training. Do you spend money teaching someone something new that will benefit the business soon, or do you spend money training someone on something he should already know? If you had a choice between sending someone on remedial training and sending someone else on advanced training, what would you do? The answer seems obvious to me.

There are some very credible reasons we would want to train our staff and they are all valid for staff who perform well. What are the reasons to train poorly performing staff? Bringing them up to the current standard of work? I do not believe this is a very strong reason to spend finite resources because it is unlikely the payback will be enough to warrant the investment. You probably won't get any value added productivity if you are not getting even the minimum required productivity, and others on the team have to pick up the slack created by the poor performer.

I think we should offer training only to those who are performing well, and we should offer underachievers or poor performers remedial training only. Even this I am conflicted about because it looks like a reward. If a poor performer gets training in a new technology, or goes to a conference, this sends mixed signals. Training is not an incentive, it is a reward and should be perceived as such. Good performers get inducements and external motivators. Poor performers should not get any external motivators or inducements because they are not bringing an acceptable level of performance to the table to begin with. For poor performers to get training is much like getting to eat dessert though you have not finished your dinner. Dessert is a treat, not a staple. Work is a staple, and not doing your job properly should not mean you get the things that people consider over and above or benefits.

Do we want people to improve? Yes. Do we want people who are performing below an acceptable standard to improve? Of course, but there is a risk in using finite resources to try to bring someone from poor to acceptable. We could also use those resources to get people from acceptable to great. What gives you the biggest bang for the buck? If your goal is to create the best team you can, which can meet its objectives, I think you have answered the question.

Ultimately, I do not believe it should be the responsibility of a company to oversee its employees' development. People need to be willing to do it themselves (i.e., show internal motivation). Companies can offer inducements for people to improve themselves via training as long as it is to the benefit of the company, but offering training to everyone on the flawed assumption that everyone improves does not really provide the most benefit to the company.

Sports illustrate this point perfectly. If the coach wants a player with better skills, wants to get rid of a troublesome player, or wants to augment the team's skill set, does he invest time, effort, and money into increasing someone's skill or making them more likeable, or does he do a trade for someone else? Trading for a new player with exactly the skills he needs is the fastest way to make a change for the better. The point is that you can make a difference almost immediately with new talent and a new attitude instead of burning time, effort, and money to improve someone's skill or personality.

Isn't a trade analogous to a termination from a particular team? The coach is the manager, and his job is to win (get results), so he tries to get the best team for the money. Does a manager in a company have a different purpose? Managers have a staff (team) that is expected to perform to an acceptable standard. The difference between business and sports is that there seems to be some professional arrogance in business that manifests as a belief that a manager is able to turn around poor performers and miraculously make them better than they really are.

Continuity of staff is important, but if a person is not adding any value, her continuity is not valuable to the company. It comes down to this: We pay employees to do a job; can they do it—yes or no? It is a very simple question, yet we tend to complicate it with ideas about intent, nurturing, providing opportunities for growth, and so on. Can they do the job? If yes, make them happy and treat them well. If no, and it is obvious they will not improve to an acceptable level, they need to be let go. If you decide to go the third route and given them time to improve, you will have nothing but complications. What happens when they improve? How long before you provide the next ultimatum? How long are you going to tolerate poor performance? That is a question only you can answer, but the longer you take, the more time, effort, and money you will lose.

Preventing Poor Performance

Don't Hire a Poor Performer

How can you recognize a poor performer before you hire him? The tests used in the hiring process give the semblance of using some sort of scientific method to weed out applicants who won't fit in with the business. I am sure the track record for these tools is good, but is it foolproof? It seems unlikely. I am quite sure people can manipulate the results to a certain extent. You cannot assume that people's answers will be completely truthful if those answers are the gateway to employment. Everyone is a team player when the question is, "Are you a team player or do you prefer to work alone?" because everyone knows that's the right answer. How valid can these hiring tests be if these types of questions are answered untruthfully? Or how invested are you in the entire process when you have canned questions and are expecting a canned answer or waiting to hear the buzzwords of the week so you can check them off a list?

People, I believe, are usually truthful, but is the person who gives the right answers on the test the truthful applicant or the right applicant? Using tools that attempt to make the hiring process objective may make HR feel warm and fuzzy, knowing they hired the "best," but you will not know how well someone performs at a job until you observe her doing the job.[2] There are some things that you cannot test. Sometimes you just get a feeling about someone, and if you do, you should probably listen to that feeling. This is not scientific or fair, but that is just the way it is. What you should take from this is very simple: hiring someone is a crapshoot.[3] There are things you can do to stack the odds in your favour, but in the end, you only really know whether you hired right when the person is in the job and performing well.

---

2   According to Frank Schmidt and John Hunger, "for hiring employees without previous experience in the job the most valid predictor of future performance is general mental ability." Schmidt, Frank L., and John E. Hunter. "The Validity and Utility of Selection Methods in Personnel Psychology: Practical and Theoretical Implications of 85 Years of Research Findings," *Psychological Bulletin*, 124(2):262–274.

3   "The process is not consistent, and you cannot get consistent results." Boydell, Janet, Barry Deutsch, and Brad Remillard. *You're Not the Person I Hired!: A CEO's Survival Guide to Hiring Top Talent*. Bloomington, IN: Author House, 2005.

Forget Your Ego

As I said, hiring people is a crapshoot. You might have done everything right and still find yourself with a poor performer. After you finish scratching your head asking yourself what happened, what are you going to do about it? You can coach the person, send him on training, or call them out on his poor performance and tell him you expect him to improve. As a manager, you have a lot of options.

One option that I have never seen used is termination within the three-month probationary period. I am sure it happens, but I have never seen it done. Why is that? If you hire someone to have skills X, Y, Z, and you find that she is not meeting your expectations, do you shrug and say "better luck next time" or do you do something about the situation?

For some people, admitting that they hired a bad employee is just too much loss of face. Others hope that with time, the employee will get better, but will he really? Are you willing to take that chance? The whole point of probation is to see whether the person will work out. If he does not, he should not continue to be employed.

I am a firm believer in admitting when I make mistakes. If a person admits to hiring a poor performer and takes action to remedy the problem, that says to me she has integrity. People will respect someone more if she admits she made a mistake and does something to correct it than if she puts Band-Aid after Band-Aid on a bad situation trying to make it better. Admitting to mistakes should not take a big person; it should be something that people just do. Despite the social and psychological issues surrounding people's behaviour, I firmly believe that it is far better to identify a poor performer you hired instead of having other managers notice the poor performer while you try to justify hiring and keeping him.

Changing Our Way of Thinking

Why Does It Take So Long to Decide to Terminate?

I have often wondered why it takes so long to decide to terminate an employee. I think part of the problem is that the phenomenon of employees suing for wrongful dismissal has been so engrained over time that companies want to establish that they have all their bases covered to protect themselves from a lawsuit. As I have shown, there is a tremendous waste of productivity and money on an employee who is not working to a reasonable standard. If she is costing the company money, let's say 20% of her salary a year in lost productivity, is that acceptable? I think any rational person would say no.

If you compare business to the world of sport and imagine employees as professional athletes, you want the best you can get for the money you are paying. If you hire someone who is continually bad and the weakest on the team, what do you do? Send him to motivational speakers? No, you give him an opportunity to improve, and if he can't or won't, you either trade him or put him in the minors.[4] Anyone who does not have what it takes is cut from the team. We expect that type of ruthlessness in our sports teams, but when it comes to business, we feel we need to find a way to get the person to improve. If the person is less skilled than the others on the market, it is pretty obvious what the next step should be. You may think this will result in a revolving door of employees who are just not up to the task, but that really should not happen, unless the company you work for has systemic problems with hiring, training, and management. It takes time and effort to train staff and to get them up to speed, and continuity of staff is essential to the smooth running of the company, so it is unlikely massive cuts will happen.

The irrational part of this thought process comes when a

4　Hockey analogy.

company refuses to spend money on removing a problem. Some people see a termination without cause as rewarding someone for being a bad employee, and refuse to do it. On some level I agree, but we are not looking at the big picture when we think like that. After we terminate the poor performer, we have the opportunity to fill the position with someone better. Productivity may falter initially, but how much of a problem is this when the person replaced was not up to the task to begin with? The staff will pick up the slack until the new person can be online and fully functioning. That is probably what they were doing since the poor performer started working in the department. Now that the poor performer is gone, things should improve and find a new normal.

Is it a waste of money to pay someone to leave? No, because this represents a resolution. It is not the same thing as throwing good money after bad. From the moment of dismissal on, the person's performance has nothing to do with anything because she is no longer with your company and reporting to you.

Do we care about whether the dismissed employee can find a new job? On a personal level, no one wants to be responsible for someone's lack of employment, but there is a limit to the manager's and company's responsibility, especially when the employee himself leaves the employer little choice by performing in a continually poor manner. If the company feels compelled to offer job counselling or job transition services—go for it.

What Are You Going to Do?

The problem I see with modern management thinking is not so much about the poor performer; it is in how we define what a poor performer is and how we then deal with poor performers. I am questioning the processes we have put in place and our rationale for doing what we do. In any other situation, people refuse to tolerate something that performs below a reasonable expectation, or their expectation. How many people have personally complained about something when it doesn't do what they think it should do? Only in business, and when it comes to people, are we somehow hamstrung by our humanity. We fail to use the same level of logic or rationality we use in other aspects of our lives to come to the hard realizations that some things just do not work and need to be replaced. It is a reality that everyone on some level experiences every day. All I am asking is why we do not we use the same logic or rational thought when it comes to a person's performance.

From the beginning to the end, I have asked very simple and straightforward questions on a very simple topic: can the poor performer meet expectations? If it is clear they cannot, there is nothing left to discuss. From where I am standing, there appears to be too much understanding, too many excuses, and not enough accountability and personal responsibility. All of this stems from one flawed assumption: that all people are capable of doing the same job to the same level as everyone else. We know that is not the case. If it were, we would not see large variations in performance, and everyone would be able to reach a stated standard without question.

We tell ourselves the cause of poor performance is some external factor that needs to be dealt with, in order for the poor performer to achieve what they have been asked to do. The reality is that we are too scared to admit that some people can and some people cannot. In fields that rely on physical per-formance, we have no problem admitting that not everybody can reach certain standards, but in fields that are about brain power, thought processes, internal motivation, thinking, com-municating, and being understood, we are uncomfortable with the reality that not everybody has the same natural ability. When people cannot do what is expected of them because of limita-tions in their natural abilities, the situation moves into taboo territory, which is impossible to address. Instead of dealing with it directly, we hold the belief that everyone can do any job and meet any standard—that everyone is equal at least in potential, when really, that never has been the case.

This is not an earth-shattering revelation. Everyone knows

this. Highly touted management books even say it quite bluntly, yet while management agreeably reads these books and nods at the concepts and has reading groups to discuss those very concepts and how the organization can implement some of these "great new ideas," when it comes to poor performance a line is drawn in the sand, and we all agree that poor performance is caused by external forces. The immediate position is that it must be an external issue that is causing the poor performance, because all employees are competent, yet no one asks why everyone else who does that same job can meet or exceed the given expectations if everything else is equal. Instead of looking at the poor performance in a vacuum, which it appears we are doing currently, we should look at it in the context of a group setting; I think we will see that all the fingers are pointing in one direction. How you deal with it is entirely up to you.

Bibliography

Academy of Management. *Organizational Behaviour Conference Paper Abstracts.* Academy of Management Annual Meeting Proceedings 2010. 8:1–171.

Allen, R. W., and David G. Griffeth. *Job Performance and Turnover: A Review and Integrative Multi-Route Model.* Human Resource Management Review, 9(4):525.

Andersson, Lynne M., and Thomas, S. Bateman. "Cynicism in the Workplace: Some Causes and Effects." *Journal of Organizational Behavior*, 18:455.

Anseel, F. and F. Lievens. "The Long-Term Impact of the Feedback Environment on Job Satisfaction: A Field Study in a Belgian Context." *Applied Psychology: An International Review*, 56(2):254–266.

Axlerod, Beth, Helen Handfield-Jones, and Ed Michaels. "A New Game Plan for C Players." *Harvard Business Review*, Jan 2002.

Ayyub, B. M. "On Uncertainty in Information and Ignorance in Knowledge." *International Journal of General Systems*, 39(4):415–435.

Baron, Robert A. "Negative Effects of Destructive Criticism: Impact on Conflict, Self-Efficacy, and Task Performance." *Journal of Applied Psychology*, 73(2).

Barr, S. H., and E. J. Conlon. "Effects of Distribution of

Feedback in Work Groups." *Academy of Management Journal*, 37(3):641–655.

Belschak, Frank D., and Deanne N. Den Hartog. "Consequences of Positive and Negative Feedback: The Impact on Emotions and Extra-Role Behaviors." *Applied Psychology: An International Review* 58(2):274–303.

Bonitz, V. S., L. M. Larson, and P. I. Armstrong. "Interests, Self-Efficacy, and Choice Goals: An Experimental Manipulation." *Journal of Vocational Behavior*, 76(2):223–233.

Boydell, Janet, Barry Deutsch, and Brad Remillard. *You're Not the Person I Hired!: A CEO's Survival Guide to Hiring Top Talent.* Bloomington, IN: Author House, 2005.

Brookhart, S. M. "Feedback That Fits." *Educational Leadership*, 65(4):54.

Brookhart, S. M. "Tailoring Feedback." *Education Digest*, 76(9):33.

Brown, K. A. "Explaining Group Poor Performance: An Attributional Analysis." *Academy of Management Review*, 9(1):54–63.

Buckingham, Marcus, and Curt Coffman. *First, Break All the Rules: What the World's Greatest Managers Do Differently.* New York, NY: Simon & Schuster, 1999.

Burson, K. A., R. P. Larrick, and J. Klayman. "Skilled or Unskilled, but Still Unaware of It: How Perceptions of Difficulty Drive Miscalibration in Relative Comparisons." *Journal of Personality and Social Psychology*, 90(1):60–77.

Butilcă, Delia, et al. "The Use of 360-Degree Feedback Method." *Annals of the University of Oradea, Economic Science Series* 18(4):300–306.

Cartney, P. "Exploring the Use of Peer Assessment As a Vehicle for Closing the Gap Between Feedback Given and Feedback Used." *Assessment & Evaluation In Higher Education*, 35(5):551–564.

Colbert, B. A. "The Complex Resource-Based View: Implications for Theory and Practice in Strategic Human Resource Management." *Academy Of Management Review*, 29(3):341–358.

Collins, F. "Career Self-Interest and Concern for Others—the Effects of Co-worker Attitudes On Fraudulent Behavior." *Accounting & The Public Interest*, 6:95–115.

Collins, James C. *Good to Great: Why Some Companies Make the Leap—and Others Don't.* New York, NY: HarperBusiness, 2001.

Colvin, Geoff. *Talent Is Overrated: What Really Separates World-Class Performers from Everybody Else.* 1st edition. Portfolio Hardcover, October 2008.

Comim, Flavio. "Capabilities and Happiness: Potential Synergies." Review of Social Economy 63(2):161–176. *Business Source Complete.* EBSCO. Web. Accessed 24 Oct. 2011.

Crisp, Beth R. "Is It Worth the Effort? How Feedback Influences Students' Subsequent Submission of Assessable Work." Assessment & Evaluation in Higher Education 32(5):571–581. ERIC. EBSCO. Web. Accessed 24 Oct. 2011.

Darke, P. R., and S. Chaiken. "The pursuit of self-interest: Self-interest bias in attitude judgment and persuasion." *Journal of Personality and Social Psychology*, 89(6):864–883.

De Dreu, C. K. W. "Rational self-interest and other orientation in behavior: A critical appraisal and extension of Meglino and Korsgaard." *Journal of Applied Psychology*, 91(6):1245–1252.

De Stobbeleir, K. E. M., S. J. Ashford, and D. Buyens. "Self-regulation of creativity at work: The role of feedback-seeking behavior in creative performance." *Academy of Management Journal*, 54(4):811–831.

Drucker, Peter F. *The Frontiers of Management: Where Tomorrow's Decisions Are Being Shaped Today.* New York: Truman Talley, 1986.

Earley, P. C. "An examination of the mechanisms underlying the relation of feedback to performance." *Academy of Management Best Papers Proceedings*, pp. 214–218.

Eisikovits, N. "Proportionality and self-interest." *Human Rights Review*, 11(2):157–170.

Ejaz, W., S. S. H. Shah, J. Aziz, A. R. Jaffari, A. Zaman, and M. R. Jaffari. "Role of self concordant goals in obtaining innovation and creativity in the employees." *Interdisciplinary Journal of Contemporary Research in Business*, 3(4):172–181.

Engle, P. "The elusive silver bullet." *Industrial Engineer*, 38(4):20.

Faulhaber, R. W. "The rise and fall of 'self-interest.'" *Review of Social Economy*, 63(3):405–422.

Fisher, Richard. "The curse of knowledge." *New Scientist*, 211(2823):39–41. Academic Search Complete. EBSCO. Web. Accessed 24 Oct. 2011.

Giovanola, B. "Re-thinking the anthropological and ethical foundation of economics and business: Human richness and capabilities enhancement." *Journal of Business Ethics*, 88(3):431–444.

Goodhew, Geoffrey W., Peter A. Cammock, and Robert T. Hamilton. "The Management of Poor Performance by Front-Line Managers." *Journal of Management Development*, 27(9).

Goomas, D. T., and T. D. Ludwig. "Standardized goals and per- formance feedback aggregated beyond the work unit: Opti- mizing the use of engineered labor standards and electronic performance monitoring." *Journal of Applied Social Psychology*, 39(10):2425–2437.

Hoogervorst, N., D. Cremer, and M. Dijke. "Why leaders not always disapprove of unethical follower behavior: It depends on the leader's self-interest and accountability." *Journal of Business Ethics*, 95:29–41.

Ibrahim, S. S. "From individual to collective capabilities: The capability approach as a conceptual framework for self- help." *Journal of Human Development*, 7(3):397–416.

Ijose, O. "Strategic human resource management, small and medium sized enterprises and strategic partnership capabil- ity." *Journal of Management & Marketing Research*, 5:1–13.

Ispas, L. "Understanding capabilities." *Revista Academiei Fortelor Terestre*, 14(2):27–34.

Jay, J. "How to get the feedback you didn't really want to hear." *American Salesman*, 56(7):21.

Jellema, F., A. Visscher, and J. Scheerens. "Measuring change in work behavior by means of multisource feedback." *International Journal of Training & Development*, 10(2):121–139.

Jones, R. G. "Review of management rewired: Why feedback doesn't work and other surprising lessons from the latest brain science." *Personnel Psychology*, 64(1):272–274.

Kagitcibasi, C. "Psychology and human competence development." *Applied Psychology: An International Review*, 51(1):5.

Kapuchinski, Stanely. "Recognizing and Taming Personality Disordered Individuals in Business." *The Journal for Quality and Participation*, 30(4):37–40.

Kim, Sang H. *1,001 Ways to Motivate Yourself and Others*. Turtle Press, 1996.

Kim, T.-Y., D. M. Cable, S.-P. Kim, and J. Wang. "Emotional competence and work performance: The mediating effect of proactivity and the moderating effect of job autonomy." *Journal of Organizational Behavior*, 30(7):983–1000.

Kline, Theresa J.B., and Lorne M. Sulsky. "Measurement and Assessment Issues in Performance Appraisal." *Canadian Psychology* 50(3):161–171.

Kosturiak, Jan. "Innovations And Knowledge Management." *Human Systems Management*, 29(1):51–63.

Krasman, J. "Taking feedback-seeking to the next 'level': Organizational structure and feedback-seeking behavior." *Journal of Managerial Issues*, 23(1):9–30.

Krueger, J., and R. A. Mueller. "Unskilled, unaware, or both? the better-than-average heuristic and statistical regression predict errors in estimates of own performance." *Journal of Personality and Social Psychology*, 82(2):180–188.

Kruger, Justin, and David Dunning. "Unskilled and Unaware—but Why? A Reply to Krueger and Mueller (2002)." *Journal of Personality & Social Psychology*, 82(2).

Kruger, Justin, and David Dunning. "Unskilled and Unaware of It: How Difficulties in Recognizing One's Own Incompetence Lead to Inflated Self-Assessments." *Journal of Personality and Social Psychology*, 77.6 (1999): 1121–1134.

Kruger, J., et al. "Why the unskilled are unaware: Further explorations of (absent) self-insight among the incompetent." *Organizational Behavior and Human Decision Processes*, 105(1):98–121. ScienceDirect. EBSCO. Web. Accessed 24 Oct. 2011.

Latham, G. P., L. L. Cummings, and T. R. Mitchell. "Behavioral Strategies to Improve Productivity." *Organizational Dynamics*, 9(3):4–23.

Lee, C. D. "Feedback, not appraisal." *HR Magazine*, 51(11):111.

Lepine, J. A., and L. Van Dyne. "Peer Responses to Low Performers: An Attributional Model of Helping in the Context of Groups." *Academy of Management Review*, 26(1):67–84.

Levine, Pamela. "Substandard Job Performance: Development of a Model and the Examination of Poor Organizational Performers". Colorado State University, 2006

Luthans, F., and S. J. Peterson. "360-degree feedback with systematic coaching: Empirical analysis suggests a winning combination." *Human Resource Management*, 42(3):243–256.

Madigan, T. "Reviving the gender agenda: A human development approach." *One in Christ*, 44(2):136–152.

Maitland, I. "The human face of self-interest." *Journal of Business Ethics*, 38(1/2):3–17.

Malandro, Loretta A. *Say It Right the First Time*. New York: Mcgraw-Hill, 2003.

Maner, J. K., and N. L. Mead. "The essential tension between leadership and power: When leaders sacrifice group goals for the sake of self-interest." *Journal of Personality and Social Psychology*, 99(3):482–497.

Manzoni, J. F., and Jean-Louis Barsoux. *The Set-Up-To-Fail Syndrome: How Good Managers Cause Great People to Fail*. Boston, MA: Harvard Business School, 2002.

Martini, R., and B.M. Shore. "Pointing to parallels in ability-related differences in the use of metacognition in academic and psychomotor tasks." Learning and Individual Differences 18.2 (2008): 237–247. ScienceDirect. EBSCO. Web. Accessed 24 Oct. 2011.

Mathieson, F. M., T. Barnfield, and G. Beaumont. "Are we as good as we think we are? self-assessment versus other forms of assessment of competence in psychotherapy." *Cognitive Behaviour Therapist*, 2(1):43–50.

Mathur, S., R. Stoll, Y. Krongold, F. Nicastro, N. Brickhouse, and M. Elvis. "AGN feedback: Does it work?" *AIP Conference Proceedings*, 1201(1):33–36.

Mattern, K. D., J. Burrus, and E. Shaw. "When both the skilled and unskilled are unaware: Consequences for academic performance." *Self & Identity*, 9(2):129–141.

McPhie, Neil A. G., and Mary M. Rose. *Addressing Poor Performers and the Law*. Mspb.gov. U.S. Merit Systems Protection Board, 29 Sept. 2009. Web. Accessed 14 Feb. 2011.

Morris, J. A., J. C. Urbanski, and J. W. Slate. "Rethinking motivation: Self-interest vs. others-directed models of human behavior." *Business Education Innovation Journal*, 1(2):74–82.

Ng, J. R., and J. K. Earl. "Accuracy in self-assessment: The role of ability, feedback, self-efficacy and goal orientation." *Australian Journal of Career Development*, 17(3):39–50.

Nhl.com. "NHL Records Held or Shared by Wayne Gretzky" http://www.nhl.com/ice/news.htm?id=384583.

Northcraft, G. B., A. M. Schmidt, and S. J. Ashford. "Feedback and the rationing of time and effort among competing tasks." *Journal of Applied Psychology*, 96(5):1076–1086.

Olalla, M. F. "The Resource-Based Theory and Human Resources." *International Advances in Economic Research*, 5(1):84–92.

Overeem, K., H. Wollersheim, E. Driessen, K. Lombarts, G. R. Grol, and O. Arah. "Doctors' perceptions of why 360-degree feedback does (not) work: a qualitative study." *Medical Education*, 43(9):874–882.

Parham, Creda Pamler Joe. "The Construct of Substance Abuse Enabling Applied to Poor Performance Management: How Managers Deal with Poor Performing Employees." PhD diss., Virginia Polytechnic Institute and State University, 2003.

Penny, J. A. "Management rewired: Why feedback doesn't work and other surprising lessons from the latest brain science by Charles S. Jacobs." *Personnel Psychology*, 64(3):816–820.

Pesta, B. J., D. S. Kass, and K. J. Dunegan. "Image theory and the appraisal of employee performance: To screen or not to screen?" *Journal of Business & Psychology*, 19(3):341–360.

Peter, Laurence J., and Raymond Hull. *The Peter Principle*. New York: W. Morrow, 1969.

Pfeffer, Jeffrey, and Robert I. Sutton. *Hard Facts, Dangerous Half-Truths, and Total Nonsense: Profiting from Evidence-Based Management*. Boston, MA: Harvard Business School, 2006.

Phillips, J. "The role of excess cognitive capacity in the relationship between job characteristics and cognitive task engagement." *Journal of Business & Psychology*, 23(1/2):11–24.

Poortvliet, P. M., O. Janssen, N. W. Van Yperen, and E. V. de Vliert. "The joint impact of achievement goals and performance feedback on information giving." *Basic & Applied Social Psychology*, 31(3):197–209.

Rocha, H. O., and S. Ghoshal. "Beyond self-interest revisited." *Journal of Management Studies*, 43(3):585–619.

Ruggiero, J. A. "Identifying and developing high potential leadership talent." *Journal of Personal Finance*, 7(2):13–33.

Sadri, Golnaz, and S. Seto. "Max performance feedback." *Industrial Management*, 53(1):14.

Sánchez Cañizares, Sandra M., and Tomás J. López-Guzmán. "The Relationship Between Level of Education, Organizational Commitment and Job Satisfaction: An Analysis in Hotel Establishments in Andalusia (Spain)." *Acta Turistica*, 22(1):37–63.

Sansone, C., and D. B. Thoman. "Interest as the missing motivator in self-regulation." *European Psychologist*, 10(3):175–186.

Schmidt, Frank L., and John E. Hunter. "The Validity and Utility of Selection Methods in Personnel Psychology: Practical and Theoretical Implications of 85 Years of Research Findings," *Psychological Bulletin*, 124(2):262–274.

Serrien, D. J., R. B. Ivry, and S. P. Swinnen. "The missing link between action and cognition." *Progress in Neurobiology* 82(2):95–107. ScienceDirect. EBSCO. Web. Accessed 24 Oct. 2011.

Shaw, Janson D., Brian R. Dineen, Roulian Fang, and Robert F. Vellella. "Employee-Organization Exchange Relationships, HRM Practices, and Quit Rates of Good and Poor Performers." *Academy of Management Journal*, 52(5):1016–1033.

Shive, Cody B. *Technical Management With Situational Leadership*. The Arrington Group.

Silverman, S. B., C. E. Pogson, and A. B. Cober. "When Employees at Work Don't Get It: A Model for Enhancing Individual Employee Change in Response to Performance Feedback." *Academy of Management Executive*, 19(2):135–147.

Soriano, D. R. "Can goal setting and performance feedback enhance organizational citizenship behavior?" *Academy of Management Perspectives*, 22(1):65–66.

Sparr, J. L., and S. Sonnentag. "Fairness perceptions of supervisor feedback, LMX, and employee well-being at work." *European Journal of Work & Organizational Psychology*, 17(2):198–225.

Sparr, J. L., and S. Sonnentag. "Feedback environment and well-being at work: The mediating role of personal control and feelings of helplessness." *European Journal of Work & Organizational Psychology*, 17(3):388–412.

Sutton, Robert I. *Good Boss, Bad Boss: How to Be the Best . . . and Learn from the Worst*. New York: Business Plus, 2010.

Taggar, S., and M. Neubert. "A cognitive (attributions)-emotion model of observer reactions to free-riding poor performers." *Journal of Business & Psychology*, 22(3):167–177.

Taptiklis, T. "After Managerialism." *Emergence: Complexity & Organization*, 7(3/4):2–14.

U.S. Merit Systems Protection Board. "Removing Poor Performers in the Federal Service," p.8. Available at www.mspb.gov.

Van Fleet, D. D., T. O. Peterson, and E. W. Van Fleet. "Closing the performance feedback gap with expert systems." *Academy of Management Executive*, 19(3):38–53.

Vogt, C. P. "Maximizing human potential: Capabilities theory and the professional work environment." *Journal of Business Ethics*, 58(1–3):111–123.

Vuolevi, J. H. K., and P. A. M. Van Lange. "Beyond the information given: The power of a belief in self-interest." *European Journal of Social Psychology*, 40(1):26–34.

Walker, Melanie. "A human development and capabilities 'prospective analysis' of global higher education policy." Journal of Education Policy 25(4):485–501. Academic Search Complete. EBSCO. Web. Accessed 24 Oct. 2011.

Waseem, M. "Relative importance of pay level satisfaction, career development opportunities, and supervisor support in perceived organizational support." *Journal of Yasar University*, 5(19):3264–3277.

Watson, G., and F. Sheikh. "Normative self-interest or moral hypocrisy?: The importance of context." *Technical Report 3*.

Widmann, Nancy C., Elaine J. Eisenman, and Amy Dorn Kopelan. *I Didn't See It Coming: The Only Book You'll Ever Need to Avoid Being Blindsided in Business.* Hoboken, NJ: John Wiley & Sons, 2007.